Something for Everyone

MEMORIES OF
Lauerman Brothers Department Store

MICHAEL LEANNAH

Wisconsin Historical Society Press

Wide view of Dunlap Square, with Lauermans on the left | *Bob and Eva Kiefer*

"*I think about tomorrow
and wonder why it is
we give up all the things
we love the most.*"

—Utah Phillips

Published by the Wisconsin Historical Society Press
Publishers since 1855

© 2013 by the State Historical Society of Wisconsin

wisconsinhistory.org

Printed in the United States of America
Designed by Shawn Biner, Biner Design

17 16 15 14 13   1 2 3 4 5

Library of Congress Cataloging-in-Publication Data
Leannah, Michael, 1957–
  Something for everyone : memories of Lauerman Brothers Department Store / Michael Leannah.
    p. cm.
  Includes index.
  ISBN 978-0-87020-581-1 (cloth : alk. paper) 1. Lauerman Brothers Department Store. 2. Department stores—Wisconsin—History. I. Title.
  HF5465.U6L385 2013
  381'.1410977533—dc23
                            2012026938

This book is dedicated to my father,
Francis X. Leannah,
and to all who ever worked
at Lauermans Department Store.

Frank Lauerman III

Contents

Preface

WHEN MY FATHER SPOKE of "the store," no one misunderstood. He meant Lauermans. When Mom said, "Your father is at the store," we knew he wasn't out buying groceries. Around our house, when someone spoke of "the store," we saw the words in capital letters: The Store.

But the word *store* can't begin to capture the essence of Lauermans Department Store. The usual image of a turn-of-the-twentieth-century "general store" is hardly a match for the magnificent building in the heart of Marinette, Wisconsin. On the store's fiftieth anniversary, in 1940, the *Marinette Eagle-Star* newspaper stated: "It is difficult to find in cities twice the size of Marinette, a store [that] has four floors and blankets an entire city block." Lauermans was by far the largest retail building north of Green Bay. To the people of northern Wisconsin and Michigan's Upper Peninsula, it was a virtual palace, a sight to behold. Drawing near made one's heart skip a beat.

More than a mere history of the store, this book is a salute to the people who were there behind the counters, on the delivery trucks, walking the aisles. Over the years, Lauermans sold a tremendous amount of merchandise, but those interviewed had little to say about the goods that were sold or the sales that were made (malt cones excepted). Invariably, the preferred topic was the people who worked and shopped there and how the store affected their lives. While a fortunate few were able to recall the 1930s and '40s, most people focused their memories on the '50s, '60s, and '70s. Those contributing information from the 1980s did so mainly "for the record"; the store by then had lost its sparkle.

My father, Francis X. Leannah, worked at Lauermans for nearly fifty years. He began on August 18, 1933, as a teenaged stock boy and clerk and worked his way up to be the manager of several departments. His wife and all six of his children were employed there for varying lengths of time as well.

Lauermans was doing well at the time of my father's death, less than a year after his retirement in 1980. That he didn't have to witness the hard decline and closing of the store that meant so much to him is a blessing. It is for him, mostly, that I have written this book.

"No monument was ever built for your father in Marinette," says Frank Lauerman III. "But there are a million little ones. He shaped an awful lot of what Lauermans became. To many people, he *was* Lauermans Store."

Let this book be his monument.

I interviewed close to a hundred people for this book and asked many questions of each of them. Many of them asked me a single question in return: "Why do you want to write a book about Lauermans?"

My answer was always the same: Lauermans was a special place. Its story demands documentation, and the people who worked there deserve recognition and commemoration.

If there are errors on these pages, I hope they are few. Puzzle pieces contributed by individuals with firsthand knowledge didn't always fit with those of others who also were there. Even newspaper accounts and other historic documents contained discrepancies. Back when the memories were being made, no one expected a book to be written about them. (Though if you had a 1910 nickel's worth for every time a Lauermans clerk uttered the phrase, "Someone oughta write a book about this place," you'd have enough to buy—and fill—every piggy bank that ever graced a shelf at the store.)

No one kept accurate notes, so the story of Lauermans as presented here can hardly be considered complete. But the hundred-odd people I interviewed for this project provided a cumulative account of this place called Lauerman Brothers Department Store. Their memories tell the story.

In all honesty, someone should have written this book in 1970. Much has been lost in the mists of time since then. But folks remain who remember that wonderful store. People everywhere speak wistfully and with near reverence about the department stores of their youth, and Lauermans is no exception. Indeed, people love talking about Lauermans, and once they start, they don't want to stop. The Christmases, the Friday nights, the normal, humdrum Tuesday afternoons—all are fondly recalled.

The people and events that made Lauermans what it was indeed deserve to be remembered. I hope by the end of this book you will agree.

(**Note:** After the business changed its name from Lauerman Brothers to Lauermans, an apostrophe was sometimes—but not always—used (Lauerman's). Some well-known department stores used an apostrophe (Macy's), while others did not (Gimbels). In this book I refer to the store as Lauermans; I use an apostrophe with the Lauerman name only to indicate possession.)

Acknowledgments

I am grateful to the following people who, with much kindness and patience, gave assistance to this project. Their help is immensely appreciated.

Amber Allard of the Menominee Historical Society, Donna Barribeau, Deb Bauer, Elsie Mae Bauer, Jane Behnke, Jeff Behrendt, Virginia Bilodeau, Jerry Blohm, Karen Boron, Chuck Boyle, Chuck Boyle Jr., Tom Boyle, Ann Buscher, Ruth Cahill, Dawn Carviou, Jane (Champley) Christenson, Marianne (Hoffman) Conlan, Larry Ebsch, Mary Edmondson, Jean Eggener, Ed Embertson, Dave Engel at the Oshkosh Public Library, Mary Falkenberg, Carol Faucett, Fannie Fillinger, Chuck Finnessy, Steve Fulford, Pamela Garcia at the Waupun Public Library, John Garon, Terry and Mary Girard, Steven Grace, Jerry and Bonnie Haines, Ethel Hannot, Richard Harbick, Warren Heider, Bonnee Lee Heim, James Hermsen, Alice Hinz, Jennifer Hollihan of the Farnsworth Public Library in Oconto, Judy Hopfensperger, Bob and Eva Kiefer, Joe Kiefer, Dorothy Kitzinger, Sam Komp Sr., Mary Ann Langill, Dick Larson, Chris Lauerman, Henry Lauerman Jr., Jim and Maureen Lauerman, Jay (Frank IV) Lauerman, Joseph A. Lauerman Jr., Geralyn Leannah, Joan Leannah-Brumm, Patrick Leannah, Vonciel LeDuc of the Manistique Historical Society, Sandy Loberg, David Lundgren, Gregory Maccoux, Sandy Mathy, Susan McAllister, Sally McGee Zander, Ila Moede, Martha Mogensen, Dr. Thomas Neumeyer, Glen Nordin, Verda Otten, Bonnie Paulsen, John and Carol Payne, Helen Peterson, Jenny Peterson, John Plouff, Dorothy (Parent) Pronold, Manette Raboin, Dave and Janet Remington, Lorraine Renton,

Rob Romero, Lori Rose of the Delta County (Michigan) Historical Society, Dan Ryan, Rita Sadowski, Howard R. Schleis, Patricia Schroeder-Burton, Mary Schuchart, Jim and Sue Schwiebert, Barbara Skorija, Paul J. Smith, Frank Smoot, the research staff of the Stephenson Public Library in Marinette (including Janet Glime and Mariel Carter), Joy Story, Jennifer Swanson, Margaret Swanson, Kathy Thill, Dan Trippler, Mary J. Von Heimburg, Karen Waloway of Northland Village in Marinette, Jaci Peterson Yoap.

Employees of these libraries and historical societies were extremely helpful: Appleton Public Library, Appleton Historical Society, Hedberg Public Library (Janesville), La Crosse Public Library, L. E. Phillips Memorial Public Library (Eau Claire), Madison Public Library, Marathon County Public Library (Wausau), McMillan Memorial Library (Wisconsin Rapids), Milwaukee Public Library, Racine Public Library, Superior Public Library, Waterloo (Iowa) Public Library.

Thanks to Kurt Steidl, Rob Becker, Jody Korch, and editor Terry LaSelius of the *Marinette Eagle-Herald* newspaper and to Jim Strickland and Nancy Engberg for technical support.

I owe so very much to Kate Thompson, my editor at the Wisconsin Historical Society Press. Working with such a supportive, open-minded, and skillful editor was a real joy. I greatly appreciate Kate's enduring faith in this project. To her and to all the staff members at the Wisconsin Historical Society Press who helped bring life to the pages of this book, I am forever grateful.

I am especially indebted to Betty Sladek, Joan Alfredson, Bruce Leannah, and Frank Lauerman III. This book would not have been possible without the special help and mounds of information provided by these kind and knowledgeable individuals.

Delivery wagons on Vine Street behind Lauerman Brothers (undated). The men and their horses are primed and ready for action. Note the interested workers in the viaduct window and on the store's window ledges. | *Menominee Historical Society*

Introduction
A Day in the Life of Lauermans

IN THE 1970S, a developmentally disabled man known to all simply as Harry frequented the music department at Lauermans. The white-haired little man (if you were five feet tall he looked up to you) walked quickly, as if perpetually late for the bus. Harry's routine never varied: He'd scurry to the record racks and select an album to buy, usually something from the easy listening racks. When Harry appeared at the counter with his selection, the clerk, under orders from department manager Frank Lauerman III, jotted the price ($5.98 in those days) on a slip of paper taped to the front of the album.

Harry would reappear two or three times a day to lay down his earnings from sweeping sidewalks or shoveling snow—two nickels, a quarter, and three pennies at 1:30, three dimes and a penny at 4:15—and watch as the clerk reduced the amount on the slip.

"How much now?"

"Three dollars and twenty-nine cents."

"That's not bad," he'd say, and off he'd go as fast as his legs would take him. He'd continue this way, whittling the price down until he owned the album, which usually took him several days to accomplish. Then he'd return to the racks to select another and start the cycle over again. (If there are any retail outlets today that allow a customer to pay for merchandise on the "Harry-style" installment plan, I'd like to know.)

Now follow Harry as he leaves the second-floor music department—better pick up your pace—down the back stairs, past the candy counter, and out the door to the Vine Street sidewalk. Let Harry be on his way and fasten your attention to the next person coming in the door. Whether it's a customer, an employee, or one of the Lauermans themselves, chances are this person's business will be as interesting as that of our friend Harry, for Harry was just one of the storied individuals populating the Lauermans scene.

Most of the customers were regulars, known well, as much a part of the fabric as the employees. They *belonged* at Lauermans. An early ad read: "A Price to Fit Every Purse," and indeed the store offered something for everyone. From shoes to furniture, from dishes to apparel, Lauermans stocked the best name brands from Chicago, New York, and Europe for those whose pocketbooks allowed for such. On the other side of the aisle, people scrabbling for a living found shirts with stitching

The jewelry department in the early 1920s. In 1935 the floor was resurfaced with the beautiful marble most people today remember. | *Frank Lauerman III*

slightly cockeyed on the sleeves, or books with crooked printing on the cover. It wasn't beneath the richest man in town to
walk into Lauermans, while right beside him, and feeling just
as comfortable, entered a woman from the other side of the
tracks in search of fabric scraps with which to make clothes for
her children.

Lauermans, like all good department stores, always
seemed busy—it looked busy, felt busy, *was* busy. Every day, a
large percentage of people in the Marinette/Menominee area
found themselves within the walls of Lauermans at one time
or another. A quick stop for a box of pencils, some fish hooks,
a pair of woolen socks. A studied search for just the right mat-
tress, sofa, or washing machine. On a cold winter day, a stroll
through the store on the way to the bank or to the dentist was
always a good idea. For employees, shifts of eight or ten hours
were on the daily schedule. Hundreds of people came together
every morning, each playing a part in the grand symphony that
was Lauermans. Let's imagine a typical day in 1970, when our
friend Harry was a member of the orchestra . . .

One clerk drives in from Porterfield in a dilapidated
pickup truck. Another, in a gleaming Lincoln Continental, ar-
rives from Marinette's west side. A third rumbles in from the
Old Peshtigo Road in a Dodge Charger. (They park up Liberty
Street or behind the public library, leaving the spaces in the
Lauermans parking lot for the customers.) A married couple,
wishing the Twin City Bus still ran, hoofs it across the bridge
from Menominee. Someone else comes walking from her home
on Wisconsin Street. A man pedals his bike up Riverside Avenue. More cars arrive—from Coleman, Wallace, Menekaunee,
Shore Drive, Water Street, Carney Boulevard. This is how the
army of employees gathers each day at the Lauermans building
at the corner of Main and Dunlap in Marinette.

The maintenance crew clocks in at six, just ahead of the
lunch counter help. The Lauermans themselves are in their

Manager Francis X. Leannah (in background, without hat) and clerk Mary Mathy (far right) assist customers in the crockery department in the early 1950s. | *Michael Leannah*

offices by the time the managers arrive, between seven thirty and eight. Clerks and stock people punch the clock at eight, an hour before the retail day begins. Display lights are turned on. Money is counted and deposited in the cash registers. Merchandise is straightened and readied. Nine o'clock. A loud buzzer sounds to alert the troops, and the store is open for business.

Within minutes the operation is in full swing, workers and shoppers like bees in a buzzing hive. Customers clamor for attention, asking questions, plunking merchandise on the counters, opening their purses and wallets. Public-address announcements break the hum of the murmuring voices, the chiming cash registers, the click-clack of stenographers' typewriters. The aroma of bacon wafts into the shoe department from the adjacent lunch counter area. The switchboard flickers like a Christmas tree as the operator plugs connections to the paint department, men's furnishings, stationery.

The fabric department, first floor (undated). Adrienne Schacht is the clerk at left. | *Joan Alfredson*

Delivery trucks roar to life, warehouse managers shout to the help, the elevator operator's call echoes in the air. A salesman sits across a desk from men's wear manager Chuck Boyle, leaning forward and plying him with this month's deals. The sales clerk in crockery waves to her friend in the camera department. A customer hefting an enormous shopping bag filled with shoes and underwear and envelopes and bolts of cloth sighs as she waits for the long-winded man in the telephone booth near the door at Dunlap Square.

At ten o'clock a mother scolds her boys fighting over a shiny red truck in the toy department. A number of managers meet for coffee at the lunch counter, joined, as they are each day, by friends from neighboring businesses. A dish falls in crockery and someone grabs a broom. Maintenance is called to the music department to coax electricity from an outlet that's gone dead. In the print shop, a worker stacks a new batch of scratch pads, glue still soft. Phones ring, crates roll, clerks say thank you, and customers leave well satisfied.

Beginning at eleven o'clock, employees cover for each other as lunches are taken. Clerks cluster in booths at the lunch counter, ordering grilled cheese sandwiches, hamburgers, bowls of chicken noodle soup. Workers with bag lunches find quiet corners in the basement locker area or in the second-floor lounge. Some of the managers (Francis Leannah, Ray Lauerman, and Norm Harpt, to name but three) take a quick lunch, then meet for their daily card game ("Smear") at the tables in the tavern inside Goodfellow's Store across the square. Other managers go home for a brief nap.

All employees are back in force by two o'clock. The advertising manager sits at his desk and looks over the layout for tomorrow's newspaper ad. Two clerks open a shipment in school supplies and begin sorting the pens of different colors. For the second time in less than a year, installers lay new carpeting in front of the ladies' ready-to-wear counter; business has been that good. In a small office adjacent to the music department, Frank Lauerman III helps an elderly woman in the purchase of a hearing aid. When a little boy tips his malt cone too far to the left and the best part falls to the floor with a splat, a waitress hurries to get him another, quelling his horrified wail.

A young man signs a check at the furniture counter; he and his wife are now proud owners of a five-piece bedroom suite, to be delivered tomorrow morning. Maintenance is called to perform its magic on the warehouse freight elevator, which won't move from its position eighteen inches above ground level. Manager Harold Pierce places a charge slip into the dumbwaiter basket, pulls the rope, and presses the buzzer; the cashier in the office will take it from there. A clerk at the hardware counter heckles the guy over in appliances, who dishes it right back; a customer in housewares smiles at the sound of their laughter. Meanwhile, in a second-floor office overlooking Dunlap Square, Jim Lauerman interviews a candidate for a secretarial position.

"Who's that new guy in the shoes?" the paint department clerk asks at the lunch counter. "His name is Bill," says the waitress through a cloud of cigarette smoke. "And he leaves a nice tip." A woman in ladies' ready-to-wear tries on her ninth dress;

the clerk dutifully hangs each rejected piece back on the rack. Someone tells a really good joke in the furniture department; the clerk in carpeting leans his ear to the laughter, wishing his customer would hurry her inspection of the rug samples he's laid out. Down in cameras, a teenaged girl rips open an envelope and gawks at the newly developed photographs, just in.

A public-address announcement informs late shoppers that it's ten minutes to five. Purchases should be made; the store is about to close. Clerks gather receipts and bag the money; the numbers had better match up when it's counted minutes later in the office on the third floor. Shortly after five, the punch clocks in the dingy hall at the east end of the basement clack and clang. The day's work is done for this drove of workers.

Now the cleaning crew goes to work, sweeping, mopping, polishing, preparing the store for tomorrow. To bolster this week's check, a clerk from hardware grabs a broom and joins his friends from maintenance. They finish as early as eleven o'clock sometimes but often are there until 1 or 2 a.m. Then for a few hours the store is dark, empty, and still. In an earlier era, a solitary night watchman remained on duty until the sun peeked out again in the morning, in time to see those arriving for the new day.

By 1970 the night watchman had long since gone the way of the store's fire stoker, tobacconist, and milliner. The presence of such individuals, however, remained in the memories of dozens of people still working at Lauermans who had been there in the 1940s or earlier and who could tell their young counterparts that, yes, those were the days . . .

A Brief History of the Department Store

Several nineteenth-century European merchants, some in business as early as 1820, laid claim to founding the world's first department store. The establishment most authorities recognize as the very first of its kind, however, is the Bon Marché in Paris, founded by Aristide Boucicaut in 1838. Boucicaut's

shop initially dealt strictly with the sale of fabric, known as piece goods or yard goods, and later branched into women's clothing, millinery, and shoes. By 1850, the Bon Marché had developed into what would later be called a department store. (The first recorded use of the term *department store* appeared in 1887 in an advertisement by what had formerly been called H. H. Heyn's Clothing Store in New York.)

Boucicaut bucked the merchandising trends of his era with such groundbreaking innovations

Aristide Boucicaut, founder of the Bon Marché in Paris | *The Grand Emporiums: The Illustrated History of America's Great Department Stores* as mixing items like stockings and handkerchiefs in the same store (in the 1830s, preachers railed from the pulpit against such practices); encouraging browsing (prior to Boucicaut, customers felt obligated to buy *something* before leaving a store); tagging all items on display with fixed prices (a practice that put an end to the age-old rule of "Never pay the first price asked"—no more haggling with clerks); issuing money-back guarantees; and reversing the long-standing tradition of taking high profits on goods that turn over slowly. Boucicaut bought cheap and sold cheap, in large quantities.

Small shopkeepers complained that the "department store octopus" would come to devour everything in its path. One small store advertised in the 1850s: "It is better to have a thousand storekeepers fairly prosperous than two or three millionaires and 997 bankrupt tradesmen." Some larger stores were firebombed, and their owners occasionally received threatening letters. The animosity toward the owners of large stores continued for years; later entrepreneurs including Marshall Field and John Wanamaker often surrounded themselves with bodyguards.

From 1860 through 1910, the number of department stores in the United States increased prodigiously. When as a consequence the price of urban real estate surged, merchants began building up instead of out, and soon department stores in many cities dwarfed the buildings around them. The stores were the centers of their communities, and the owners, embracing the role of civic leader, often posted a code of ethics by which the store promised to do business—and by which they urged their patrons to live as well. (See the Lauerman Brothers' code of ethics, page 177.)

Alexander Turney Stewart is considered to have been the owner of the first American department store. Beginning with a small shop in New York, Stewart moved to increasingly larger quarters, culminating in 1862 with the Cast Iron Palace

Stewart's Cast Iron Palace in 1898, two years after it was purchased by retail mogul John Wanamaker | *The Grand Emporiums: The Illustrated History of America's Great Department Stores*

at Broadway and Tenth Street in lower Manhattan, the "largest store in the world." Mary Todd Lincoln enjoyed shopping there, eventually redecorating the White House with goods purchased entirely from Stewart's. Not a bad endorsement.

After several business deals met with failure, the persistent Rowland Hussey Macy finally found success with a New York dry-goods store. In 1866 he expanded his business for the first time by buying the building next to his. He continued to expand until he owned the entire block at Sixth Avenue and Fourteenth Street in Manhattan. In 1902, Macy's established its flagship store at Herald Square, again buying up adjacent properties until it occupied the entire block, this time minus the lot at the corner of Thirty-fourth Street and Broadway, giving the store the distinctive look it still has today. Macy didn't live to see his establishment at its peak (nor did later co-owner

3

Macy's Manhattan department store in 1904 | *Macy's: the Store, the Star, the Story*

Isidor Straus, who went down with the *Titanic*). In 1924, at 2.2 million square feet of floor space and employing more than eleven thousand workers, Macy's called itself the biggest store in the world.

Adam Gimbel began with a trading post in Indiana, expanded to Milwaukee in 1887, then to Philadelphia in 1894, and finally to New York in 1910. There, a spirited competition between Macy's and Gimbels would persist for years. (Gimbels, by the way, held the first Thanksgiving Day parade in Philadelphia in 1920, four years before Macy's got into the act.)

Gimbels retained its hold as a retail giant until 1973 when it was sold to BATUS, Inc., who continued to use the name Gimbels on the stores. In 1986 Marshall Field's took over Gimbels' cornerstone in downtown Milwaukee. In 1997 Field's closed the Milwaukee store.

Gimbels' original downtown Milwaukee store, circa 1905
| *WHi Image ID 53376*

John Wanamaker, once dubbed the "Greatest Merchant in the World," began business in Philadelphia in 1861. His innovations in advertising intrigued and delighted customers. An especially successful campaign involved helium balloons sent afloat; anyone presenting a found balloon was rewarded with a new suit of clothes. Wanamaker's new store in 1876—all one story—was the largest retail space in the world, lighted by stained-glass skylights during the day and gas chandeliers at night. Wanamaker made waves by hiring women, promoting a shorter workday, and offering high wages, insurance, and pensions. His store housed a school to help employees complete their grade school educations.

While Marshall Field's wholesale division was led by John G. Shedd, who took the reins of the entire company after the death of Marshall Field in 1906, Harry Gordon Selfridge (right) headed the retail side. "Mile-a-Minute Harry," born in Ripon, Wisconsin, helped bring Marshall Field's to its height in the 1890s. Some sources credit him with coining the phrase "the customer is always right." Selfridge left Field's in 1904. In 1909 he established Selfridges Ltd. in London, the first of a chain of high-end department stores in the United Kingdom. | *WHi Image ID 45848*

A young Marshall Field went to work for P. Palmer & Company four years after that business's inception in 1852. With partner Levi Leiter, Field bought out Palmer in 1865. After more buyouts—and name changes—the store called Marshall Field & Co. opened in 1881. With more show windows than any business establishment in the world, Marshall Field & Co. was not the biggest, but it was the grandest. Field's even sent its elevator operators—including a young Dorothy Lamour—to charm school.

Strawbridge and Clothiers, Bloomingdale's, Woolworths, J. L. Hudson's, J. C. Penney's, and other leading department stores had strengths and qualities of their own. Every store clamored for a reason to boast, to single out its winning attributes. The businesses continually jockeyed for position as the biggest, the tallest, the one with the most employees, the one that used the most electricity or the most bricks in its construction.

The title "World's Largest" didn't remain long with the one bold enough to claim it. In the book *Service and Style*, Jan Whitaker wrote that the Philadelphia store John Wanamaker built in 1911 could have held an entire 125,000-square foot "big box" store of today on each of its fourteen floors. Robert Hendrickson in *The Grand Emporiums* used a different way to describe the immensity of the "Largest": "A good sized house has 2,000 square feet of living space, so you could put 10,100 houses in Macy's" in New York.

All the big operators of the late nineteenth century knew how to draw in crowds. Stewart's offered continuous organ music for shoppers. Wanamaker's Philadelphia store contracted with Thomas Edison in 1878, and the store was the first to have its interior lit with the newly invented electric lightbulb. Merchants enticed customers with free babysitting, wheelchairs for the old and infirm, and ventilation fan systems. Wanamaker's had a "sick room" with a doctor in attendance. They were also the first to provide an in-store restaurant and to offer visits with Santa Claus at Christmastime. Some stores had supervised playground facilities with pools, sandboxes, merry-go-rounds, and zoos, so mothers could engage in carefree shopping.

Pie-eating contests brought in curious onlookers, as did high-wire acts and human fly demonstrations. One store offered delivery by parachute. And lessons of all sorts were available. When bicycles reached peak popularity in the 1890s, stores hired experts to teach customers how to ride. Others sponsored beauty clinics, fashion shows, parades, dog shows, and dancing competitions. Celebrities made appearances, politicians gave speeches, and authors read passages from their latest books. Customers flocked in for demonstrations of new inventions and technology: pneumatic tubes, telephones, hydraulic elevators. In the 1800s, in-store concerts were popular; later, radio stations broadcast programs on the premises.

Nearly all the stores offered floor walkers to assist customers. (One store listed 113 different duties assigned to its floor walkers.) Children younger than ten commonly worked as cash runners and messengers, chasing from department to cashier and back. These "cash children" ceased to be needed after the invention of the pneumatic tube system, implemented first at Wanamaker's, in 1880. Macy's came to boast of twenty-four miles of pneumatic tubing and claimed that one of its brass cylinders traveled twelve thousand miles on a busy day.

Though the buildings differed greatly in exterior architectural style, the interiors were remarkably alike. The order of the day called for a wide main aisle on the first floor, high ceilings, mezzanines, glass showcases, and marble floors and columns. The ground floor was always the most luxurious, with deluxe lighting and detailing and ceilings up to ten feet higher than those on the upper floors.

Early research showed that shoppers tended to stay on the first floor, often within fifty feet of the entrance. This knowledge led to trends in department layout accepted by nearly all of the big stores. Jewelry, cosmetics, candy, notions, and men's clothes were found on the first floor. (Men, being reluctant shoppers, needed this accommodation.) Women's and children's clothing, underwear, fabrics, toys, and crockery were on the upper floors, with furniture and carpeting always on the very top. Dry goods and discount clothing were relegated to the basement.

Children were virtually invisible in the early department stores. The focus was always on the adults, particularly women. With the exception of underwear and socks, children's clothing was typically still made at home. Toy departments were given little space, except at Christmastime, when they were temporarily expanded.

With elevators able to hold only a small number of people at a time, many customers found shopping on the upper floors inconvenient. The escalator—also called "moving stairway" or "inclined elevator"—was invented as a novelty and introduced at a Coney Island amusement park in 1896. The Otis Elevator Company purchased the patent and developed the escalator for practical use. The new invention opened the upper floors of retail establishments to more shoppers. (Down escalators were not considered necessary at the time.) The first department store to install escalators was Bloomingdale Brothers' at Third Avenue and Fifty-ninth Street in New York.

Though air-conditioning still belonged to the distant future, at the turn of the twentieth century improvements in department store air quality became necessary. Customers and clerks alike commonly fainted, especially in the stuffy basements. The paper fans distributed to customers on hot days alleviated the problem minimally, at best. The summer heat also caused candy, candles, and soap to melt and stick together. Ventilating fans and cooling and humidifying systems gave moderate relief. Though theaters and restaurants took to air-conditioning in the 1920s, most department stores went without until the 1950s, and then installed it for the first floor only.

Remembering Lauermans

"On really hot days, the only way to keep the store cool was to open all the doors and hope a breeze blew in. Imagine today the security problems with doing such a thing."
—*Former clerk Chuck Finnessy*

Before the days of radio and television, department store advertising consisted primarily of newspaper notices and the store's display windows. In the early 1890s, large front windows became a must. Stores on a corner, facing two streets, had a distinct advantage over establishments in the middle of the block. With curious customers gathering on the sidewalks to see what's next, display design became an art. Again, stores were constantly trying to outdo the competition—and themselves. A single window could have more than five hundred items laid out in elaborate patterns. Live animals were often featured as part of a display, and of course Santa Claus played a big part in December.

Though largely unnoticed, the roots of the decline of the department store started to take hold in the early 1930s. After the Great Depression, people demanded value over style. Stores took to making alliances with manufacturers, agreeing to sell one brand only in exchange for a low wholesale price. The 1930s saw stores with high stock and few customers. The next decade brought an improving economy, and willing customers with money in their purses and pocketbooks clamored for deals. But with the war came shortages and rationing. Certain metals, fabrics, and rubber goods were in short supply, leaving some department store shelves empty. When a store did procure a shipment of blouses or kitchen items, customers snatched them up.

This sellers' market reversed the trend of slipping sales that department stores had seen in the 1930s. As prosperity surged in the postwar years, the market continued to favor department stores. The baby boom brought with it even greater demand for furniture, clothing, and other material goods. This change in fortune was short-lived, however.

As suburban populations increased in the 1950s, people became more dependent than ever on the automobile. Traffic and parking problems in city centers had businesses scrambling to build stores in outlying areas to accommodate suburban shoppers. In addition, a demand for ever-cheaper goods opened the door to newly available global markets. No-frills discount stores and specialty stores dealing strictly in furniture, toys, shoes, or appliances became the order of the day.

Remembering Lauermans

"I remember walking to Lauermans from our West End home in Menominee to Bridge Street [now Nineteenth Street], across the small dike on the Menominee River, to the side of the Interstate Bridge hill. From there we climbed up the old board steps to the bridge walkway and over to Lauermans. Sometimes we used the old iron train bridge's small board walkway to cross to Riverside Avenue and then on to Lauermans. The walk back home was tougher—we had packages to carry." —*Local historian Larry Ebsch*

Throughout the 1950s well-established department stores tried to keep up with the trends by opening branches farther and farther from the mother stores. And by 1960 a store without branches, a one-of-its-kind, was an oddity.

The nationwide rush to the suburbs did not affect Lauermans, situated as it was in a town of twelve thousand people. But the rise of the discount store did. The practice of buying cheaply in big lots—a mainstay of Lauermans since its inception—was being usurped by the upstart discounters, making it difficult for Lauermans to land favored merchandise.

Department store owners—the Lauermans included—found themselves facing some very difficult facts. In 1900 department stores did up to 90 percent of the retail trade in many American cities. In 1959 the number nationwide had fallen to 7 percent. And this was before Wal-Mart, Kmart, and Target reared their heads starting in 1962. Already gone from the scene were the in-store photographers, dry cleaners, manicurists, notary publics, library branches, and radio stations. Now, to keep up with the discount store explosion of the 1960s, most department stores were forced to discontinue free delivery, gift wrapping, holiday parades, and other extras. With the ending of such amenities, a sense of loss descended on the former giants of the industry. It would never lift.

Shopping had once been a daylong outing, not a chore but an experience people planned for and looked forward to. A department store excursion allowed for a glimpse at the outside world, a chance to be a part of the bustle. The days of shopping in the morning, having lunch in an elegant tearoom, attending a knitting class or fashion show, then carrying your bags and memories back home again are gone. But for a time—a time now seen as much too short—there was something known as the golden age of the department store. And for many of us in northern Wisconsin and Upper Michigan, that meant Lauermans of Marinette.

2

The Rise of the Lauerman Brothers

Six children were born to Joseph and Antoinette Lauerman on their farm outside the small southwestern Wisconsin town of Muscoda. Joseph Albert John came first, in 1866. Frank followed three years later. In 1870, Henry was born; he lived just twelve days. Anna arrived in 1871, Charles in 1874, and then Marie in 1876. The three boys—Joe, Frank, and Charlie—would one day be known as the Lauerman Brothers of Marinette.

According to family lore, Joe started work at age twelve as an apprentice in a Muscoda print shop. He may also have been employed for a time at Jacob Bremer's general store just down the street. What is known with certainty is that both Joe and Frank Lauerman found employment in their midteens at the general store of McDonald and Son in downtown Muscoda.

The boys clerked and cleaned, prepared mail, made deliveries, took stock, and hauled goods to and from the railroad depot. They observed how their boss dealt with area farmers arriving daily with butter, eggs, and poultry to sell. And they began to dream of someday running a business of their own.

Mail was the lifeblood of the general store, so the train schedule determined the length of the boys' workday. The mail came in on the St. Paul Railroad line three times a day—the early delivery before 6:00 a.m. and the last at 8:45 p.m. Neither Joe nor Frank shied away from hard work—or long hours. Each saw his salary increase from fifteen dollars to a respectable forty-five dollars per month.

Legend has it that among the shipments from New York arriving at McDonald and Son were those from the firm of the renowned blind wholesaler Charles Broadway Rouss. In his shipments, Rouss often included intriguing instructions for young clerks on how to go into business for themselves. Whether the Lauermans were indeed influenced by Rouss is uncertain; what is known for sure is that the Lauerman boys saved their money, kept a watchful eye on the operations of a general store, and put their heads together in the evenings when the work was done, forever discussing plans for the store they would open together.

In 1887 Donald McDonald (the "son" in McDonald and Son) traveled north to the lumber boomtown of Marinette, Wisconsin, and he liked what he saw. He returned to Muscoda

A bird's-eye view of Muscoda, Wisconsin, in 1879. Several large commercial buildings from the days of the Lauerman brothers still stand on North Wisconsin Avenue. | *WHi Image ID 22647*

Joseph A. J. Lauerman, circa 1896
| *Frank Lauerman III*

Frank Lauerman, circa 1896
| *Frank Lauerman III*

and, with his business in decline, sold as much of his merchandise as he could. Packing what remained into wagons, he and right-hand man Joe Lauerman headed for Marinette. We can only imagine the extent of twenty-one-year-old Joe's reluctance to make this move and leave his family behind.

Upon seeing Marinette, Joe immediately wrote to Frank. The place was a goldmine, he said, a bustling town with unlimited business potential. Joe urged Frank, now tied to Muscoda as town treasurer, to try doubly hard to save his money. Frank responded positively, but with not enough urgency to suit his brother. "Someday we'll make a move" wasn't what Joe wanted to hear. He foresaw problems with McDonald's business approach and wanted to break away—now. This colossal opportunity wouldn't last forever.

After Frank traveled to Marinette and saw for himself what his brother had described, the two would-be entrepreneurs advanced their plans precipitously. The potential for business in rapidly developing Marinette was undeniable. The Lauermans had $1,100 saved between them.

That would be enough.

In 1853 Marinette's population stood at 478; by 1860 the lumber boom had started, and the number of people in the growing community passed 3,000. By 1890, 11,500 people lived in Marinette. The city could boast of eight lumber companies, sixteen hotels, two hospitals, and twenty-nine saloons. A new city hall and courthouse had been built, as well as an opera house and a street railway. The newspapers published in Marinette included the *Eagle*, the *North Star*, the *Twin City Lumberman*, and the *Argus*. Also available were the Swedish-language *Forposten* and the *Marinette Tribune*; two Danish papers, the *Freja* and the *Fremad*; and a French daily, *Le Courier*.

The Wisconsin State Gazetteer and Business Directory of 1897–8 listed Marinette's population at 15,500 and boldly predicted even better things to come: "The almost unlimited forests of pine, hemlock, maple, ash, basswood, rock elm, etc., that abound in the vicinity, makes this city a formidable competitor for second place in population in the State during the next decade."

The Menominee River with a Marinette lumber mill in the distance, circa 1900
| *WHi Image ID 78839*

The *Gazetteer* reads like a yellow pages of yesteryear. The business listings were brief and to the point: *Olson, Swen milk 7 miles west.* A quick perusal reveals a number of antiquated businesses surfacing with regularity: carriage dealers, midwives, harness-makers, bikesmiths. There were thirty-six grocery stores in the Marinette area, fifteen on Main Street alone. And that's not counting bakeries or meat and fish markets. (Today there are two grocery stores in Marinette, though one might suppose that all fifteen of the turn-of-the-century Main Street establishments could fit inside either of the supermarkets in business today.)

The town rose and fell with the logging boom, which reached its zenith in the late 1890s. In 1900 Marinette's population reached 16,195. At the time, two dozen sawmills lined the Menominee River. This was the scene at the start of the Lauermans' run.

The lumber boom would come to an end, with the last of Marinette's sawmills closing in 1931. For nearly a hundred years, however, Lauermans would ride the wave created by that boom.

Today it's an empty lot in a neglected part of downtown Marinette. But in 1890, 1515 Main Street was the site of the Savings Bank Store, precursor to Lauerman Brothers Department Store. (The Savings Bank was in the former Louis Gram building, immediately east of the Colonial building, which was razed in 2008.)

While in the employ of Donald McDonald, Joe Lauerman made important connections in the Marinette business community. Competitors balked at his idea to open a store of his own, saying there were already too many stores in the area. Joe Lauerman rejected their opinions.

In 1890 Frank Lauerman made a written offer to buy out McDonald's business in Marinette. When the offer was refused, Frank made it clear to McDonald that if he didn't comply, the brothers would start their own business in a different location in Marinette. No one knew better than Donald McDonald of the Lauerman brothers' diligence and drive; he knew he wouldn't be able to compete against them. A deal was struck. Promising weekly payments, the Lauermans bought a half-share of McDonald's business for $1,500. McDonald remained with the firm as a limited partner. So began the business known as McDonald and Lauerman on April 20, 1890.

McDonald was eventually eased out of the partnership, and the business became Lauerman Brothers' Savings Bank (later simply The Savings Bank). The name played on the idea that trading there was the same as putting money in the bank.

The Savings Bank Store, Main Street in Marinette, 1890s | *Frank Lauerman III*

Notice of Dissolution.

Notice is hereby given that the partnership heretofore existing between Donald McDonald and Jos. A. J. Lauerman, under the firm name of McDonald & Lauerman, has been, on this 20th day of January, 1892, dissolved by mutual consent. Jos. A. J. Lauerman and Frank J. Lauerman have purchased all interest of Donald McDonald in said firm, and will continue the business under the firm name of Lauerman Bros. Lauerman Bros. assume all liabilities of the old firm of McDonald & Lauerman, and money due to the latter firm must be paid to them. MARINETTE, WIS., Jan. 20th, 1892.

DONALD MCDONALD,
JOS. A. J. LAUERMAN.

This 1892 notice was given with every purchase at Lauermans to announce the change in ownership.
| Frank Lauerman III

In 1891 Frank Lauerman left Muscoda to take a role in the management of the store in Marinette. Joe's and Frank's dissimilar personalities complemented one another. Joe was the more social of the two, always looking for a hand to shake and ready with a smile and a friendly word. Frank was cerebral and reticent, a good decision maker, and good at managing money. People liked dealing with the brothers, who paid their debts promptly and whose growing reputation for fairness was well earned. Customers appreciated the way the two *listened*; they paid attention to what their customers said and gave them what they wanted.

The store outgrew its modest 25-by-80-foot floor space, and in 1893 the brothers expanded their operation by renting the building's upstairs quarters and basement. By 1894, the business had grown to the point that they needed additional help, and younger brother Charles was summoned from business dealings in Idaho. Joe and Frank owned a thousand shares of company stock apiece. Each of them gave Charles a hundred shares, thereby establishing ownership ratios of 900/900/200.

Charles J. Lauerman, circa 1896
| Frank Lauerman III

The Lauerman business appeared in a notice in the 1897 edition of the Marinette *Gazetteer*. The brothers would rise in prominence to the point that people in Marinette took care to spell their name correctly. | *Michael Leannah*

By 1896 the brothers expanded further to adjacent buildings to the east and west. Initially the Lauermans had limited their business to dry goods, clothing, millinery, carpets, and crockery. Now they had ample space—and enough capital—to increase the variety of their inventory.

When the store was young, much of the merchandise was displayed outside each day, carried to the sidewalk in the morning and back inside at day's end. The brothers worked from dawn until dark and beyond, one or the other sleeping in the store on a cot under the stairway. Both Joe and Frank waited on customers and kept track of the stock. Each, however, had particular duties to tend to: Frank did the buying and Joe kept the books.

There was one well-documented exception to this arrangement. Joe made the very first buying run to New York, leaving Marinette with nine hundred dollars in currency carefully sewn into his belt. Years later he related the story of how, while between trains at the depot in Chicago, he was approached by a man who offered to sell him a cheap ticket to New York. The man led Joe into a seedy tavern and tried to coax him into a dice game and to indulge in smoke and drink. Joe ran for it. He firmly believed later that had he succumbed to the man's urgings, he would have lost all his hard-earned money and the store in Marinette would never have come to

Lauermans constructed this arch in front of their store for a special event in the mid-1890s. The city of Marinette allowed it to stay in place over Main Street for several weeks.
| *Frank Lauerman III*

be. Joe made it to New York, where he succeeded in procuring from the wholesale houses a sizable amount of stock for his money, plus more bought on credit.

Thus began the Lauerman practice of buying for less and selling for less. The brothers went over the receipts at the end of each day and placed an order to a wholesaler for replacement merchandise. They bought with cash and worked on a cash-and-carry basis, content with small profits and quick turnover. The Lauermans sold at a little above cost, while their competitors—their most prominent business rivals being Lewis Brothers on Dunlap Square in Marinette and the Kirby Carpenter Company across the river in Menominee, Michigan—stuck to their higher prices and larger profits. And fuller shelves.

Remembering Lauermans

In July 1901, Lauermans invited customers to observe a "Silk Worm Display" in the dry-goods window. "They are just beginning to spin and can be seen feeding and spinning. You can see silk in every stage from the beginning to the finished product in many fancy dress silks, novelties, and other articles. It is very interesting and can be seen here all this week." —*Marinette Daily Eagle*, July 16, 1901

The Lauerman brothers had a knack for supplying high-quality, low-priced merchandise that fit the desires of the people of Marinette. Frank made weekly trips to Chicago, where he trolled for bulk bargains on goods sold by financially troubled establishments, partially damaged merchandise, or goods from companies destroyed by fire. (For more than sixty years, Frank personally selected much of the merchandise sold at Lauermans.) Joe handled all correspondence, wrote the advertising for the newspapers and circulars, and came to do some of the buying as well. The brothers' business instincts served their partnership well, priming them for their next step: the construction of a new store right in the heart of Marinette's downtown.

Isaac Stephenson was born in New Brunswick, Canada, in 1829. He moved to Wisconsin at the age of sixteen and settled in Marinette in 1858. A prominent lumberman and landowner, Stephenson served in many political positions, including stints in Washington as both congressman and senator.

Stephenson took a liking to the industrious Lauerman brothers and in 1900 included them in his plan to remake Dunlap Square in downtown Marinette. Already gracing the square were the stately Marinette Hotel and the Dunlap Square Building. Stephenson bought the city band shell and had it torn down to make way for a public library he would donate to the city. Just one thing remained: Stephenson wanted people coming over the bridge from Michigan to see something truly spectacular. To complete his vision for the square, he needed a magnificent retail center at the corner of Dunlap and Main.

Ike Stephenson purchased the buildings between Main and Vine facing Dunlap Square—the Wilson Block, the Joe

Dunlap Square in Marinette, 1917. Lauermans is on the left. | *WHi Image ID 38618*

Fisher building, the Wright Brothers building, and the Charles Waters building. Then he sold the buildings, with the stipulation that they be moved to other locations.

Despite its numerous expansions, the Lauermans' Savings Bank Store on Main Street had again become cramped and crowded. The brothers had been looking for better accommodations, but Stephenson's proposal overwhelmed them. With all their money tied up in their inventory, they weren't able to finance the building of a new store from scratch—and certainly not the kind Ike had in mind.

Stephenson offered to finance construction of the new store and then lease it to the Lauermans. The brothers opted for an arrangement in which they would pay Stephenson in increments, with the goal of eventually owning the building themselves. Indeed, within four years of the transaction, they had accomplished that goal.

At the start of the new century, the redbrick building known as the Wilson Block, standing at the corner of Dunlap and Main, housed Addison Fairchild's drugstore, a restaurant and confectionary owned by Daniel Madigan, and Marinette's first telephone exchange. (It was also home to Dana's Third Regimental Band, of which Frank Lauerman was a member.) The entire building was lifted and moved one block south to a lot owned by Daniel Madigan and Frank Lauerman, partners in numerous business ventures. (Jerry Blohm, a longtime Lauermans employee, states that this land was purchased from his grandmother, the legendary Native American "Queen" Marinette, for twenty dollars. "Frank showed me the deed and where she signed it," he says.)

Some say that when the Wilson Building was rolled on logs to its new location, not a window cracked and not a brick moved out of place. But another story says that prior to the move, the footings at each corner had to be broken with careful blasts of dynamite. Three of the footings cooperated, but the

Men working on the road in front of the Queen City Hotel, where Ludington Street emerges at Dunlap Square. Taken shortly before the building of the Lauermans' new store, this picture shows the Wilson Block on the site of the future Lauermans store. The Wilson Block was moved over one block to become Lauermans' wholesale building and later the store's warehouse. | *Frank Lauerman III*

The Wilson Block was lifted and rolled on logs. | *Frank Lauerman III*

stubborn fourth one stayed intact even after a second try with a single stick of dynamite. An impatient Dan Madigan supposedly then used three sticks of dynamite and blew the corner off the building, sending bricks flying for blocks.

The moving of the Wilson Block cleared the way for construction of the new store. Ike Stephenson commissioned architects to design a building more majestic than any north of Milwaukee. The original plans called for a two-story building to cover about two-thirds of the area that the store eventually came to occupy. By the time construction began, however, Frank Lauerman told Stephenson that the store as planned was not going to be big enough for what the brothers envisioned. Stephenson agreed to amend the plans to accommodate three floors. (This change was later evident in the different pillar styles on the third floor.)

Remembering Lauermans

*"*Interior work will be well underway in the new Lauerman block this week. . . . Excellent progress was made on the construction work this month, the weather being very favorable. . . . The brick work is practically completed today. The steam fitters and electricians will begin work this week. . . . The glass for the windows is expected tomorrow.*"* —*Marinette Eagle-Star,* November 10, 1903

In 1904 ads for Lauermans referred to the new building on Dunlap Square as "the Big Store," to distinguish it from the Savings Bank Store up the street. For the people of Marinette watching the construction, there was no confusion. This was truly a *big store.* A *magnificent* store. Anticipation became excitement. It wasn't the first time—nor would it be the last— that Lauermans would be the talk of the town.

The *Daily Eagle-Star* reported on April 18, 1904: "In order to make preparations for the GRAND OPENING Thursday, the Big Store will be closed all day Wednesday, April 20. At 7:00 p.m. the store will be open to visitors until 10 p.m., but no goods will be sold during that evening. Music from 7 to 9. Come and bring your friends with you. Souvenirs for 'friends and patrons' ordered from Japan six months ago at considerable expense— one to each family."

With the new store came a new name for the firm: Lauerman Brothers. This notice in the *Daily Eagle-Star* announced the opening to take place on April 21, 1904. | *EagleHerald Publishing, Inc.*

Lauerman's Store, Marinette, Wis.

The new "Big Store" on Dunlap Square, 1904 | *Bob and Eva Kiefer*

The building's interior was bedecked with flowers and palms, many sent by well-wishers at other area businesses as well as suppliers and associates in Chicago and beyond. As for the aforementioned music, "Prof. Amsden will render some of his solos that made him famous in Springfield, Massachusetts, followed by Amsden's Orchestra, Frank Vandenberg, leader." The musical program consisted of marches, cornet solos, operatic selections, and more.

The Big Store opened with fifty-three departments. Some of the advertised prices seem impossibly cheap today: couches ("steel-constructed, with fancy velours") sold for $5.95; kitchen cabinets ("two bins, two drawers, two kneading boards, fancy carved legs and trim") went for $4.95.

"Now we expect to do even better," the newspaper notice intoned, "for the following reasons: Having higher ceilings and excellent light from three sides of each floor, we reduce our lighting expenses. We will save on our insurance bill. We will save the rent on ten warehouses. And we will be able to buy goods in large quantities at better spot cash prices."

Though some people did cast doubt, saying such a grand store for the "shawl-trade" couldn't succeed, in the first year on Dunlap Square the Lauerman brothers more than doubled their business. Two hundred people were employed, and five horse-drawn delivery wagons made two rounds every day.

On the occasion of the store's twenty-fifth anniversary in 1915, the *Marinette Eagle-Star* reported that "the success and rapid advancement of the firm is almost without precedent in business annals. The great success is due solely to the able management and business acumen of the proprietors, who have labored unswervingly to please their patrons in every particular."

The Lauermans purchased a thirty-nine-foot section of property east of the store, on which they built a three-story addition in 1914. They also bought the only remaining property on the block, the Marinette House at Main and Liberty, and there built a one-story annex. For five years this building served as a meeting place for the Marinette Rotary club. In 1922 a final expansion pushed the store's east wall all the way to Liberty Street, across from the former O. A. Haase shoe store. The area of the store now totaled well over 100,000 square feet and completed the building that stands today. (Evidence of the

Remembering Lauermans

"Lauerman Bros. are doing an extensive mail order business. Every morning they receive a big batch of orders from towns along the line and through the upper peninsula. They also send a large amount of goods to the island villages in Green Bay. They recently received an order from Seattle, Wash., for a diamond ring, which they filled." —*Marinette Daily Eagle*, September 14, 1897 expansions endured inside the store, in differing posts in the basement and flooring in the office on the third floor.)

So in 1922 the building was complete, standing as it does today. In 1926, however, Frank Lauerman began an expansion of the business of a different sort, through the acquisition of stores in Wisconsin, Iowa, and Michigan's Upper Peninsula. The number of satellite stores would grow to fifteen in the 1930s and then dwindle to three by the 1970s. In the end, the one left standing, the one that outlived Gimbels and other giants, would be "the Big Store" on Dunlap Square.

3

The Lauerman Family

THE LAUERMAN BROTHERS—Joe, Frank, and Charlie—were like gears that meshed very well. Each brought his own personality and skills to the business; each contributed to make it work. Together they had all the qualities needed for success: personality, intelligence, and ambition.

In the 1880s, when the boys were of school age, most farm families didn't put much stock in education beyond a basic knowledge of reading and arithmetic. All three boys left school very young. Yet this trio of brothers, with little in the way of formal education, started a business and made it thrive through instinct, hard work, and sheer determination.

Joseph A. J. Lauerman

An outgoing man, fair and generous, Joe Lauerman was much admired by the people of Marinette. Everybody seemed to like Joe.

The *Peshtigo Times* newspaper described Joseph Lauerman as a devoted family man, well loved, and charitable: "Never was an appeal to the poor made in vain to him, and frequently

Joseph Lauerman with his wife, Cecilia, and family, circa 1912. The children were, from left to right: Henry, Joseph Jr., Ursula, Catherine, Antoinette, and Elizabeth (in chair).
| *Joseph A. Lauerman Jr. Family*

he anticipated and lent a helping hand when need was great. His great charity was one of the many luminous marks that made life brighter for him and for innumerable others."

After the death of his first wife, Amelia Besio, Joe married Cecilia Kellerman in 1901. They had six children: Henry, Catherine, Antoinette, Joseph Jr., Elizabeth, and Ursula.

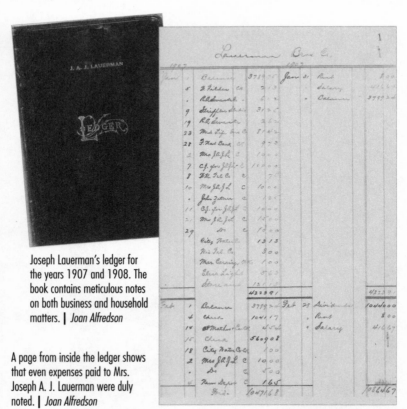

Joseph Lauerman's ledger for the years 1907 and 1908. The book contains meticulous notes on both business and household matters. | *Joan Alfredson*

A page from inside the ledger shows that even expenses paid to Mrs. Joseph A. J. Lauerman were duly noted. | *Joan Alfredson*

When he was in his forties, Joe Lauerman's health began to decline, forcing him to work fewer hours. He suffered a stroke in 1915 and another on October 17, 1918, from which he never fully recovered. Joseph Lauerman died on Saturday, December 30, 1922, at the age of fifty-six. In a tribute published in the *Menominee Herald-Leader* newspaper, Roger Andrews, owner of the paper, declared: "Neither the hardships of his early beginning in business nor the rewards which came in his successes of later years changed his personality one whit. He was ever a plain-living and plain-thinking man.... He was a man of deep religious convictions, of broad liberality, and of high ideals. Selfishness was not in him."

On the day of Joseph Lauerman's funeral, thousands of people—rich and poor, of all faiths and of every rank and class—visited his home on Riverside Avenue to pay their respects. Flags throughout the city of Marinette were flown at half-mast, and many stores and institutions remained closed in his honor. Hundreds of people attended the funeral mass at Our Lady of Lourdes Catholic Church. The funeral procession was a full mile long.

The *Menominee Herald-Leader* of January 2, 1923, noted: "No merchant in the world, great or small, was closer to his patronage, or enjoyed the distinction of knowing as many of his customers by their first names."

Four days later, the *Herald-Leader* quoted Joe Lauerman's will: "Religion to me has always appeared as the greatest force for good in the world, and while personally I have always been a follower of the Roman Catholic Church faith, I realize that all churches are striving for the advancement and betterment of mankind. In recognition of the good they are all doing, I hereby bequeath . . ." A list followed of cash bequests to Catholic, Protestant, Jewish, Christian Science, and every other religious body in Marinette and Menominee, including the Salvation Army.

Frank J. Lauerman

Though his brother Joe came first to Marinette and established the business on Main Street that became Lauerman Brothers, it was Frank ("F.J.") Lauerman who presided over the firm for nearly seventy years, guiding it with a steady and knowledgeable hand.

Frank Lauerman, 1940
| *Frank Lauerman III*

My father, Francis Leannah, spoke with great respect for F.J. when he referred to him as the Old Man. Frank was more serious and subdued than either of his brothers. His good qualities may not have been apparent to the people who thought of him as reserved, or even stern. Jim Lauerman, grandson of Frank, says, "He was six-foot-two, and he always wore a dark suit. He could be quite imposing." Longtime Lauerman employee Betty Sladek adds, "He instilled a little fear." Joe Kiefer, manager of the store's paint department for nearly forty years, says of Frank, "He was very distinguished looking. He could have been president of the United States."

Opinions differ, but the following can be stated with certainty: Frank Lauerman was a fair and generous man and was well respected in the community.

He took the dealings of Lauerman Brothers very seriously. Frank Lauerman III remembers, "When I traveled to

Chicago for a buying run with my grandfather for the first time, he told me, 'Remember: You represent Lauermans' store, so no fooling around.' This was business."

Frank Lauerman Sr. had a quiet way about him and led by example. Known for his frugality, he wouldn't stand for light-bulbs being left on unnecessarily. And he was a notorious string saver. Jim Lauerman says, "We had balls of string that would go around the world twenty times. In the transfer department in the basement, where things were wrapped, the girls down there had string balls coming out of their ears." My brother, Bruce Leannah, remembers our mother telling the story of what happened on one of her first days working at the store. "They used to wrap garbage and tie string around it before throwing it out. Mom used too much string one day and got scolded by Frank."

> ### Remembering Lauermans
>
> "Frank was the real backbone to the store. He had a very dignified air about him. . . . He was a class act. And his son was just like him."
> —*Dorothy Pronold*

Elsie Mae Bauer, longtime Lauermans employee, recalls, "Mr. Frank Lauerman Sr. would come walking down from the lunch counter and stop to say, 'Girly, turn the lights off. It's bright enough in here.' He'd go to the end of the store and come back and say, 'Girly, turn on the lights. It's too dark in here.' Later, he'd come again and say the same thing."

Jerry Blohm remembers a morning early in his Lauermans career when Frank Lauerman walked up to him: " 'Are you chewing gum?' he asked me. I told him I was. He said, 'When nine o'clock comes, that gum better be gone, or you're not working here anymore. We don't do that here.' He came down later and saw that I wasn't chewing. He didn't give me a wink, but he gave me a look. I was okay."

Frank Lauerman married Nellie Faun in 1893. They had five children: Joyce, twins Marshall Raymond (Ray) and Faith,

> ## Remembering Lauermans
>
> "The [Lauerman Brothers firm] reflects the sterling character of Frank J. Lauerman, devoted to his business and the welfare of the city of his adoption, active in every civic project, a director of many important Marinette and Wisconsin enterprises." —*Menominee Herald-Leader,* April 17, 1942

Frank Jr., and Lucille. Nellie Faun died in childbirth in 1903. Frank married Margaret Quilty twelve years later.

F. J. Lauerman's love of fishing led to the establishment of the Lauerman lodge in Wausaukee, where he often entertained friends and associates, including Kerman, Bass, and other Chicago jobbers from whom he made purchases regularly. But Frank never found the time for full retirement. He worked into his late eighties, continuing his weekly trips to Chicago to do the buying for the store. The business was his hobby as well as his life's work.

Frank Lauerman's accomplishments outside the family business are too numerous to list. Active in many community organizations, he held directorships at the First National Bank of Marinette and at the Badger Paper Mills in Peshtigo. He was a member of the board of directors of the Old Line Life Insurance Company. He financed many area business ventures, including the Bijou Theater and the Marinette and Oconto Knitting Mills. With his son Frank he acquired holdings in the Burns Department Stores of Michigan's Upper Peninsula.

Frank J. Lauerman died on May 21, 1959, at his home at 383 State Street. He was eighty-nine years old. The line of people waiting to pay their respects at the wake in his home extended out the door and down the block.

The *Marinette Eagle-Star* ran an editorial tribute to Frank Lauerman two days after his death. It read in part:

Frank J. Lauerman was the last of three Lauerman brothers whose coming to Marinette from Muscoda had a tremendous impact on the city's economy. As the Lauerman Brothers Company advanced, so did the rest of the business district. The confidence of the Lauerman brothers in Marinette instilled confidence in others. . . . The death of the elder brother, Joseph, at a comparatively early age left Frank J. Lauerman at the helm and the continuing growth of the business was almost legendary. . . .

To many, Mr. Lauerman was an austere man who appeared to take little interest in others, except for a few close, personal friends. Actually, he was a very charitable individual and there are almost countless persons who can attest to acts of kindness bestowed upon them by Mr. Lauerman in a seemingly casual manner. He took a personal interest in the sorrows of others and was among the first to lend a helping hand to those in grief. Mr. Lauerman had a strong character and great ability, the combination of which almost invariably is a big asset to any community. Marinette is the better for his good influence.

Charles J. Lauerman

The youngest of the three Lauerman brothers, Charles ("C.J.") Lauerman came to the business with qualities all his own. His business sense may not have been as strong as his brothers,' but he had a remarkable way of connecting with people. F. J. Lauerman spoke often of his envy for Charlie's easy way of talking with the customers.

Charles Lauerman was a farmer. He was working a farm in Idaho in 1894 when his brothers called for him to join them in Marinette. Even after becoming a partner in the business,

Charles J. Lauerman, 1940
| *Joseph A. Lauerman Jr. Family*

Charles farmed a property west of Marinette, raising crops and flowers as well as chickens, cows, pigs, and a prize bull.

"Charlie was a wonderful man," says Frank Lauerman III about his father's uncle. "Everyone liked him. He knew everybody." Indeed, the *Marinette Eagle-Star* once noted that "Charles Lauerman probably knows more Marinette and Menominee county farmers by their first names than does any other single person."

"Charles Lauerman made a lot of business for that store," says Joe Kiefer. "He knew the farmers. He'd go up to every farmer who came into the store and shake their hand and talk with them."

Remembering Lauermans

"I remember as a little kid seeing Charles Lauerman buy a barrel of pickles from a farmer." —*Betty Sladek*

Charles married Emma LeBlanc on April 23, 1901. Daughters Helen and Alice were born in 1902 and 1906. A son, Charles F. Lauerman, died in 1917 at the age of four. Active in a number of community and civic organizations, Charles Lauerman was the driving force behind Camp We-Ha-Kee, a Catholic girls' camp on the shore of the Green Bay near Marinette, recognized as one of the finest girls' camps in the Midwest.

Charles J. Lauerman died on the Wednesday morning of November 8, 1950, at his home at 1964 Stephenson Street. He was seventy-six years old. He had suffered a series of heart attacks over the eight months prior to his death. On Friday, the day of the funeral, the doors of Lauerman Brothers Department Store stayed closed until noon. By order of Marinette mayor Richard Murray, the flag at city hall was flown at half-mast in Charles J. Lauerman's honor.

The Lauermans were like royalty in Marinette. When one of them walked down the street, people stopped to watch. Area residents felt that Lauerman Brothers was their store, and they were always interested in newspaper accounts of any developments involving the business. There was also an appetite for news, great or small, concerning the doings of the family. Lengthy articles, such as the account of Joe Lauerman's wedding to Cecilia Kellerman on February 14, 1901, or the news of the couple's move into the new Riverside Avenue house on April 21, 1910, were common. So, too, were small news items on the inner pages:

> *Daily Eagle*, December 16, 1899: "Mr. and Mrs. Frank J. Lauerman on Thursday gladly welcomed to their hearts and house another winsome babe, a daughter."

NEW CAR ARRIVES

New Car of Frank Lauerman is the Largest in the Twin Cities.

MACHINE IS FULLY EQUIPT

Is a Six-cylinder Machine and Has Fifty Horsepower—Sixteen Feet in Length.

Frank Lauerman of this city received his new automobile today. The machine was received at the Poyer garage in Menominee on Wednesday evening and was equipt and delivered today. The machine, which is a Winton, is the largest machine in the two cities.

It is sixteen feet long, has six cylinders and is of fifty horsepower. The machine is of a buff grey color and has a graceful outline. It is fully equipt with top, lights, syren, and all of the equipment necessary for a machine of its size.

Among the other machines at the Poyer garage, the Lauerman car loomed up like a giant. It is doubtful, according to Mr. Poyer, if there is another machine of its size and elegance in this section of the state.

This notice made the front page of the *Daily Eagle-Star* on July 2, 1908. Not all cars of the time came with tops, lights, and "syrens." | *EagleHerald Publishing, Inc.*

Daily Eagle-Star, November 26, 1910: "A ceremony, unique in the fact that possibly it had never before been performed in Marinette, took place on Thanksgiving Day, when the residence of Mr. and Mrs. Joseph A. J. Lauerman, which was recently completed, was blest by the Rt. Rev. Bishop J. J. Fox of Green Bay. . . . The blessing was followed by a sumptuous dinner, served in several courses in the commodious and handsomely furnished dining room, Madam Schones catering."

Marinette Eagle-Star, March 26, 1915: "George Johnson, an employee in the delivery department of Lauerman Bros. store, was injured Thursday when he fell down the steps leading to the basement of the store. Johnson's right leg was badly bruised, and may be fractured, the swelling making a complete diagnosis impossible at present. Johnson was removed to his home."

Marinette Eagle-Star, February 22, 1924: "Mrs. Joseph Lauerman and daughter, Miss Elizabeth, have returned from a month's visit with relatives and friends in different cities in the southern part of the state and elsewhere. They were in Milwaukee, Chicago, Watertown, Madison, Muscoda, and Prairie du Chien. In the latter place they visited the Misses Catherine and Antoinette Lauerman, who attend St. Mary's College there."

Marinette Eagle-Star, July 21, 1927: "A peculiar accident happened this week on Shore Drive, near the cottage of E. W. LeRoy. His nephew, Paul Skinner, of Omaha, was practicing with a golf ball in the yard when the ball veered into the road and struck the windshield of a car driven by Miss Catherine Lauerman. The windshield was broken and pieces of the glass struck Miss Alice Lauerman, who was riding in the front seat with her cousin. Her face was cut in several places, but fortunately the cuts were not deep."

Remembering Lauermans

"I remember Frank Sr.'s wife had an electric car. This was in the 1930s. It was like a carriage you see in a magazine. She drove it by working a stick. I thought it was the neatest thing." —*Dorothy Pronold*

The Next Generations

The Lauerman brothers had children and grandchildren who carried on their work. While Joe Sr., Frank Sr., and Charlie took the department store to great heights without the benefit of much formal education, the later generations came to work at the store only after earning advanced degrees in business from universities such as Notre Dame and Georgetown or years of retail experience in New York and other cities.

Ray Lauerman,
son of Frank Sr., 1940
| *EagleHerald Publishing, Inc.*

Frank Lauerman, Jr.,
son of Frank Sr., 1940
| *EagleHerald Publishing, Inc.*

Henry Lauerman,
son of Joseph, 1940
| *EagleHerald Publishing, Inc.*

By the 1920s, Joe's son Henry had joined Frank's sons, Ray and Frank Jr., in taking responsibilities within the firm. The founders' grandsons—Chuck Boyle, Frank Lauerman III, Henry Lauerman Jr., and Jim Lauerman—were at the helm when the store closed in 1987.

Remembering Lauermans

"Ray Lauerman came to the office every morning with a fifty-dollar bill, wanting ones, fives, and tens, so he could spend them at the lunch counter. Every late afternoon he'd return with a fold of small bills, wanting a fifty."
—*Mary Falkenberg*

No Marinette family today piques the public's interest the way the Lauermans once did. Of course, the owners of Wal-Mart and Shopko aren't seen on the city's sidewalks or in the next pew over at church on Sunday. They're not seen on Monday mornings in the aisles of their stores, wishing customers a good day, the way the Lauermans used to do it. Unlike the business executives of today, the Lauermans were stitched into the fabric of the community of Marinette.

Over the span of the years at the store on Dunlap Square, the Lauermans were there, cordial and approachable. Those who worked at Lauermans knew the owners as human beings, not merely business executives issuing directives from above. It was one of the reasons so many employees stayed with the store for twenty, forty, even sixty years.

4

Why Lauermans Worked

THE FORMULA seems so simple. As I see it, here are the four main reasons for Lauermans' success as a business institution. Modern stores ought to take note.

Reason #1: Service

An article in the *Marinette Eagle-Star* in 1940 stated that "Lauermans caters to practically every whim of the housewife, laborer, farmer, businessman, and persons of all ages. *Service* is the key word. Sales service, credit service, delivery service, and numerous other services usually found only in towns of much greater population can be had at Lauermans."

In a day when credit was hard to come by at most retail centers, customers appreciated the easy credit obtained at Lauermans. "You knew who you could give credit to," says Frank Lauerman III. "Clerks knew everyone by name." Jim Lauerman adds, "You didn't just buy merchandise and go home and never look back. Personal service was very important."

The list of services Lauermans provided ran the gamut from knitting lessons to demonstrations of how to properly wax a kitchen floor to the prompt repair of sewing machines and appliances. A team of curtain rod installers appeared at the homes of customers purchasing draperies. There was once a full-time jeweler at Lauermans who did nothing but fix watches.

Jerry Blohm, manager of the electrical and appliance department, knows a thing or two about the services Lauermans provided. He told me,

Among many other services, Lauermans offered cold storage of furs, as heralded in this 1949 ad. | *EagleHerald Publishing, Inc.*

I started with Brownie [Alton Brown], the Maytag Man. I'd go with him on his oil can missions. On Monday mornings we'd go out and oil up the wringers and motors on customers' washing machines. I remember going to your grandma's [Blanche Leannah]. We'd oil up the machine, and she'd give us coffee and bakery. Before you knew it, we were outside helping to hang the clothes on the line. Didn't have dryers then. In those days, you did the wash on Mondays, and even if it rained, people did the wash and hung it up inside. I enjoyed those service runs. Lauermans always took care of their customers. We never charged anything for oiling the machines. We didn't do it for just anybody, though—you had to buy a lot of stuff.

Reason #2: A Wide Variety of Merchandise

WE SELL EVERYTHING was once emblazoned on the side of the Lauermans building. Were they exaggerating? Maybe just a little. "We sold everything but cars," claims Chuck Boyle. Jim

This main floor aisle in the 1910 era offered jewelry, alarm clocks, bolts of fabric, spools of yarn, and more. And there was never a shortage of able clerks on hand to assist a customer.
| *Charles J. Lauerman Family*

Lauerman states it differently: "Everything from grand pianos to peanuts." "Something for Everyone" was another phrase emblazoned in the store's printed ads, and on a daily basis that motto seemed to ring true.

With styles evolving and new inventions continually arriving, the inventory at Lauermans reflected the ever-changing societal landscape. The store once sold bulk oil, roofing material, barrels of gunpowder. There was a time when Lauermans had a large assortment of whips to choose from.

"We're in a constantly changing business," Henry Lauerman Sr. said in 1940. "Each year there have been important changes in the location of many departments and the types of merchandise offered."

Indeed, anything and everything was offered at Lauermans, and at varying levels of quality and price as well. Mary (Jansen) Von Heimberg says, "After I married, we moved to

Baltimore, then to California and to Rochester, Minnesota. I always knew that if I couldn't find it anywhere else, I'd find it at Lauermans."

"It was a great store," declares Elsie Mae Bauer, a clerk at Lauermans for nearly forty years. "There was nothing else like it. If somebody came in and asked for something, and Lauermans didn't have it, they got it. I don't know where they got it, but they would always get it." Jim Lauerman adds, "We didn't stock items to suit 90 percent of the customers, stuff that would turn over quickly. We bought for the other 10 percent. Just to satisfy customers."

Remembering Lauermans

"The very atmosphere was magical. When I was old enough to walk to Lauermans by myself, I remember having a dollar to buy a gift for my mother's birthday. Oh, the variety of things to choose from. Upstairs, downstairs, the store seemed huge to me."
—*Jane Champley Christenson*

Reason #3: Courtesy

New Lauermans clerks without sales experience were put through extensive instruction in how to deal with customers properly and politely. Little acts of kindness and courtesy went a long way. Manette Raboin, area resident and former office worker, says, "I remember an older woman in ladies' wear once said to me, 'It's such a pleasure to wait on you.' I remember thinking as I left, 'What a nice thing to say!'"

Customer courtesy didn't come naturally to all employees. Chuck Finnessey recalls a clerk who was notorious for helping customers with just his chin as he leaned on the counter. "Where are the brass tacks?" The man would lift his head and indicate the general direction with his chin. F. J. Lauerman was surely scowling down from heaven. But according to Verda Otten, the Lauermans "trained their employees for personality.

The main floor "Dress Goods and Silks" department (later known as the fabric department), circa 1910. Take a seat at a stool in front of the display case and give clerk Ella Gordon, at left, the opportunity to serve you with courtesy and care. | *Charles J. Lauerman Family*

My father [manager Joseph Kopetsky] always told the girls he wanted them clean and neat. If there was ever a problem, they were sent home."

On the occasion of the store's fiftieth anniversary, an article in the *Eagle-Star* said the owners of Lauermans "use their palatial offices for little more than cloakrooms." The owners were "merchandisers by instinct," and they and their managers modeled customer courtesy. According to the newspaper, the owners were "in personal contact with patrons, many of whom they know by first name" and "show strong interest in the welfare" of the customers. "To be greeted informally by officers of such a huge retail organization would be almost unheard of in larger cities, yet it happens to customers at Lauermans hundreds of times every day."

Employee Dan Ryan remembers a level of personal attention at Lauermans that modern shoppers no longer experience. "I bought an overcoat at Lauermans and wore it for a month. One day Emil Voscamp, the manager of men's wear, came to me and said it looked like the coat didn't fit very well. He insisted on giving me one that fit better. I don't know what he did with the one I had worn, if he sold it again or not."

Reason #4: Skill in Hiring

F. J. Lauerman and others in the Lauerman family gave much credit for the store's success to their stable of dedicated and able department heads. Of the managers present during the store's golden age, some had college degrees (John Burke, Francis Langrill, Harold Pierce), others trained at technical schools or gained experience in working at other retail centers (Dan Althaus, Hal Gerletti, Ed Kieff, Robert Laysell, Charles Neumeier, Martin Ourada), and a large number worked their way up the ladder at the store in Marinette.

Lloyd Dufresne started as an office boy in 1924 and retired as office manager more than fifty years later. Other fixtures at the store had similar histories: Walter DeVoe (salesclerk, 1911), Norm Harpt (stock boy, 1934), Joe Kiefer (warehouseman, 1928), Les LaFountain (clerk, 1923), and Rueben Schacht (salesman, 1929).

When I began research for this book, I set out to compile lists of those who managed the various departments. The lists were surprisingly short. For instance, in the ninety-seven-year history of the store, the stationery department had three managers. Louis Peters, with Lauermans from 1892 until the 1940s, gave way to F. X. Leannah, who, in 1980, was succeeded by his son Bruce, in charge until the end of the store's run. Not much of a list. And it was much the same in other departments.

The Lauermans managers, circa 1960. Top row: Charles Neumeier, Lloyd Dufresne, Ed Doran, Joe Kiefer, Norman Harpt, Francis X. Leannah, Rueben Schacht, Jack Burke, Martin Ourada; bottom row: Francis "Bucky" Langrill, Bob Laysell, Ed Kieff, Harold Pierce, Dan Althaus, Walter DeVoe, Lester LaFountain. | *Michael Leannah*

Joe Kiefer's nearly forty-six-year run at the helm in paint and wallpaper was not unusual.

In 1940 the *Marinette Eagle-Star* praised the Lauermans firm for hiring competent managers and employees: "Another factor in the success is the rallying around them of capable executives in whom they can depend immense responsibilities."

From the top down, the personnel at Lauermans was interestingly varied, a microcosm of the general population. On the occasion of the store's fortieth anniversary in 1930, the *Eagle-Star* stated: "About the store is sensed a spirit of loyalty on the part of employees not exactly understood by the casual shopper." Workers took pride in the store and understood its mission. They knew they were part of something unique.

Remembering Lauermans

"Betty Sladek was a lovely person. Really intelligent woman. And Marie Thull was brilliant. Those women were ahead to their time. In this day and age they'd be CEOs of big corporations." —*Chuck Boyle*

The *Menominee Herald-Leader* of April 20, 1935, noted, "The executive office doors are always open, and the heads of the firm spend more time on the floor than behind their desks." The relationships among owners, managers, and employees were very personal. Managers filled in for workers who were needed at the hospital for a spouse's surgery or at the school for a child's holiday program.

Frank Lauerman III remembers: "We hired such good people. Vern Wenzel, for instance, was like an ambassador for Lauermans. I could rely on him to calm down an angry customer. He'd go on a service call and take care of a customer's antenna, then sit down and have coffee with them. By the time he returned to the store, the customer was no longer angry."

Compare this approach to the only option for the unhappy consumer of today: Call an automated service line and get hopelessly lost trying to navigate your way to a live person. If you somehow latch onto one, you're likely told that there's a different number you need to call. No one's interested in hearing your complaint. No one's coming over for coffee.

5

Working at Lauermans

FROM THE VERY BEGINNING, the Lauermans seemed to have a sixth sense for hiring just the right people, in just the right mix. From sweet to gruff and everything in between, customers encountered the gamut of personalities. It's the quirky and colorful employees—not the building or the merchandise—that people most remember with fondness when they look back to the days of Lauermans store.

L. T. "Tom" Plouff was the very first Lauermans employee, starting as a clerk the week before the original store opened in 1890. Plouff became manager of the women's clothing department and remained with Lauermans until his death in 1934. Shortly before he died he wrote this account of his beginnings at Lauermans:

> One day while I was enjoying a short vacation I passed by a small building on the main street of our town and heard someone making a lot of noise, and stepping up, I looked in. And then a pleasant, smiling gentleman invited me in. I asked him what he was doing and he told me he was opening up a new store. He then asked me many questions: how old I was, where I went to school, and he ended up asking me if I would like to work for him.

I told him I was fourteen and that I attended the Union High School [later Marinette High School]. He also asked me if I intended to go until I graduated. I said no, my father said if I could get a good job I could quit.

This nice gentleman was Mr. Joseph Lauerman, late of Muscoda, Wisconsin, who was opening up the "Savings Bank Store." Well, to make a long story short, I took the job at $3.00 a week. Mr. L. told me he started the store with $1,000. You couldn't buy too large a stock with that. He had some piece goods, overalls, men's and children's stockings, gloves, tablets, pencils, crayons, ink, some religious pictures, and a few other items.

I was the first and only employee. A Mr. McDonald went in with him but quit as he said it would never pay to have two owners, that it would not succeed. Mr. Lauerman thought different.

My first job was to deliver a hanging lamp in a small express wagon. The lamp was china, the shade was trimmed with glass prisms. The city roads had high

Tom Plouff drove a delivery wagon much like this one on his first job for Joe Lauerman, transporting a fragile chandelier to a woman adept at making doughnuts. | *Frank Lauerman III*

wooden sections with large cracks in them and as I pulled the wagon the prisms kept swaying to and fro. I was afraid they would fall off or strike against the side and break, so I sat down every so often until they quit their movement. It was rather bumpy traveling on those old wooden side roads and I was glad when I arrived at my destination and could sit down and rest awhile.

I helped hang the lamp and I saw a large pan of doughnuts on the kitchen table, the product of my client's morning's work, and I eyed them fondly. She told me to take a couple, which I did, and she also gave me a couple for Mr. L. When I returned he was angry because I stayed so long, but when I told him what a hard time I had and gave him the doughnuts he said he wished I had stayed longer and brought back more doughnuts. Then we laughed and we were good friends again. But "Mr. Joe" as everyone began to call him was like that. He scolded when he thought you needed it, but then forgot about it.

Soon after, Mr. F. J. Lauerman came into the firm, as he was not old enough when Mr. Joe started. Later Mr. C. J. Lauerman became a member and they employed more clerks and I delivered with horses and delivery wagons. The store was very successful and they moved into their present store on Main Street, later purchasing it. They formed a corporation, employed about 350 people, but I was always the #1 clerk in the largest small store north of Milwaukee.

I became buyer for several departments, going to Chicago and New York several times a year. . . . I have been in Lauerman Bros. Co. now for forty-four years. I am home on account of illness—but hope to return to work soon.

Another early employee was C. L. "Louis" Peters, whom the *Eagle-Star* once dubbed "the dean of Lauerman Brothers company employees." Peters moved from Menasha to Marinette when the aunt with whom he lived relocated. He started employment at Lauermans in 1892, splitting and carrying wood, and retired more than fifty years later as manager of the stationery, toys, office supplies, crockery, glassware, novelties, and cameras.

"When a person likes his work, the years slip by quickly," Peters was quoted as saying in the *Marinette Eagle-Star* in April 1940. Peters became the Marinette postmaster after retiring from Lauermans.

C. L. Peters, 1940
| *EagleHerald Publishing, Inc.*

Candy bars once sold for a nickel and a gallon of gas all of twenty-four cents. So it's hard to put into perspective just how much—or how little—Lauermans' employees earned "back when." Many former employees look back with wonder at how they supported themselves at hourly wages of less than a dollar. Although it seems today like a pittance, most admit that the pay was at least "acceptable." And some will go further than that.

"Lauermans was good to their workers," states Mary (Jansen) Von Heimberg, niece of longtime employee Bertha Lemieux. "In the era right after the Depression, people were grateful to have jobs." Verda Otten, daughter of manager Joseph Kopetsky, concurs. "The salaries were low, I suppose, but sufficient. My father kept a charge account at the store and paid off the debt with his Christmas bonus."

In the days of Lauermans, a person's work meant more than his or her paycheck. "Your father and I had chances to work elsewhere," office manager Lloyd Dufresne told me, "but we enjoyed working at Lauermans. Never made any money, but what's money?" Lloyd started at Lauermans as an office boy in 1924, working seventy-plus hours a week for eleven cents an hour. He scrabbled his way up to office manager, overseeing the bookkeeping processes for accounts receivable and accounts payable. He counted out the cash register amounts every morning and made deposits at the bank every noon. He stopped working full-time in 1975 and retired in 1985, after sixty-one years on the job. "I never felt as if I hated to go to work in the morning," he said at the time of his retirement. "I was always glad to be up in the store."

Remembering Lauermans

"My dad, James Champley Jr., had his first job at Lauermans in men's ready-to-wear. He always spoke of his job at Lauermans with great pride." —*Jane Champley Christenson*

Indeed, the Lauermans had ways of keeping their workers satisfied—although sometimes just barely. "I always got a raise when I asked for one," says my brother, Bruce Leannah, "though it was never what I wanted. They'd give you a nickel more per hour, not the quarter that you asked for."

Ruth Cahill, later a fixture in the toys, moved from department to department in her early days at Lauermans. "I relieved George Schacht in men's wear during his lunch hour one day. F.J. [Lauerman] had gotten some pink shirts. No one wore pink shirts back then, unless they were in an orchestra or something. Well, I sold two pink shirts, and F.J. was watching. Two days later, my boss in the wholesale office [Joseph P. Lauerman] called me out and said, 'F.J. liked your spunk and how you knew how to handle people. There'll be something extra in your pay envelope this week.' You know what I got? Fifty cents. Those were the days."

Nonsalaried employees entered the building at a door near the corner of Liberty and Vine. Stairs led down to a dimly lit hallway where the punch clocks stood, near the public restrooms and employee lockers. (The beautiful wooden bulletin board that once graced this hallway can now be seen in the Dunlap Avenue entrance to the boutique occupying the main floor of the Lauerman building.) After punching in, workers filed past the maintenance area, the freight elevator, and the postal delivery office. As they emerged into the basement retail section on the way to their posts, perhaps they occasionally considered some of the fringe benefits of working at Lauermans. Full-time workers received a 20 percent discount on most store purchases. Managers and their families got 30 percent off and part-timers 10 percent. "At one time the employee discount was 10 percent over cost," remembers Glen Nordin. "You could buy the finest suit for thirty-five dollars."

Lauermans was an unusual place, says Nordin, in that the owners paid wages in cash. "They made out these little envelopes and put them in that old safe at night. It would have been easy for someone to come and blow that thing and get all that cash in those envelopes. I asked them why they didn't write out checks. Office manager Lloyd Dufresne told me, 'This way they spend money on the way out of the store.'"

For many years the employee Christmas bonus was a generous doubling of the week's pay. Later, Lauermans gave employees turkeys or gift certificates. Joe Kiefer remembers that "in Charlie Bilodeau's era, they'd put silver dollars in your pay envelope." (Bilodeau was the office manager in the 1930s and 1940s.)

At the annual Lauermans employee picnic in 1917, Edith Lahaie surprised everyone by defeating her male opponent, Max Galatz, in the one-hundred-yard dash. The *Menominee Herald-Leader* called it "a most exciting finish." Miss Lahaie later joined the team called the Suffragettes (Mazie Connors, Anna Cabana, Emma Bartels, Elizabeth Barthel, Agnes Belinke, and Flora Lahaie) to win the ladies' tug-of-war contest, pictured here. | *Menominee Herald-Leader*

Management showed its appreciation, too, every April on the event of the store's anniversary. Before 1920 Lauermans closed for a half day to allow for a gala employee picnic. With families included, up to a thousand people attended these affairs. The company provided streetcar fare for the trip to Lakeside Park (near what later became the Silver Dome resort), where guests were greeted by a rousing orchestra, food, merriment, and games.

As late as the 1930s, Lauermans celebrated its business anniversaries with separate men's and women's parties held at the Marinette Hotel. Employees were later allowed to intermingle at the Elks Club, Red 'n Ed's, or another of the area's supper clubs, where each was given dinner with a pair of cocktail tickets. Smaller gatherings took place during the holidays in the homes of employees. Best remembered are the holiday festivities at the homes of Erv Krukowski, Ray Pinkowski, and other fun-loving individuals. Lloyd Dufresne held "office personnel only" parties in his home, at which he could always be coaxed to play a song or two—or more—on the organ.

The unidentified young man receiving the gift of silverware is surrounded by many longtime Lauermans employees familiar to many yet today: Art Nelson, Joe Kiefer, Charles Bilodeau Jr., Rueben Schacht, Walter DeVoe, Alton Brown, Herb Guimond. Impromptu, in-store parties such as this one were common.
| *Virginia Bilodeau*

Dorothy Kitzinger recalls my father taking people's confessions at the company parties. "He'd sit at the end of a table and hold his handkerchief in front of his face, like the screen in a confessional. It was so funny."

Lauermans frequently saluted its employees with Clerk of the Month awards and tributes published in the local newspaper. Photos of employees were sometimes included in the advertisements, proud moments for those people.

On October 5, 1956, the *Menominee Herald-Leader* ran a lengthy account of a celebration marking Laura Parent's fifty-year association with Lauermans. Parent worked her way up from wrapping clerk to cashier to salesclerk to buyer for the jewelry, purses, and gift departments. The newspaper quotes her speech at the dinner, which took place at Red 'n Ed's Supper Club and was attended by seventy women employees: "While

On the store's seventy-fifth anniversary, Lauermans ran multiple-page ads in the local newspaper featuring pictures of many of the employees. Shown here are Millie Belaire, Marion Borgwardt, Art Nelson, and Helen Blahnik. | *EagleHerald Publishing, Inc.*

this seems to be strictly a ladies' party, may I speak of and pay homage to my first employers, Frank, Joseph, and Charles Lauerman, the latter two deceased, as always being kind and considerate. Their families have grown up while I've been there and are very dear to me, as well are the many in-laws and grandchildren and all affiliates and fellow employees." Sounds

These familiar faces at the jewelry counter are, from left to right, Gertrude LaFountain, Laura Parent, and Bertha Lemieux, seen here in the mid-1950s.
| *Mary Von Heimburg*

like the words of someone who got more than a paycheck by working at Lauermans.

For a business the size of Lauermans, some early efforts at creating employee pension funds were commendable. At one time F.J. insisted that all employees have a one-thousand-dollar life insurance policy, for which each employee paid ten cents a week. "I remember a widow stopping Frank and thanking him for that," says Jim Lauerman.

Working at Lauermans had other, more unusual perks:

- A leak developed on the roof at the base of the old flag pole, so it was taken down. Employee Jerry Blohm had purchased his first TV set in 1951 and needed a pole for an antenna. The flag pole was lying in the back of the store. Henry Sr. told Jerry he could have it. "I still have it," says Blohm.

- On more than one Fourth of July, Lenroy Sulk took a break from his evening maintenance chores to sit on the roof of Lauermans and view the fireworks being launched from Stephenson Island. He had the best seat in the house.

Alton Brown, Lauermans' "Maytag Man," demonstrated the latest in the world of refrigeration for an interested customer in the 1950s.
| *Virginia Bilodeau*

- My father, Francis Leannah, was responsible for maintaining the gum ball dispensers and weight machines on the staircase landings. Every month or so he brought home cloth sacks full of pennies and dumped them on a card table in the living room. The family had great fun pawing through the coins looking for collectibles. Those kept were replaced with coins of the same face value.

By and large, Lauermans workers showed great loyalty to their employers, the best testament being the large number of people who remained with the store for a quarter of a century or longer. It must be said, however, that at times this loyalty was mistakenly assumed. Dan Ryan, who worked at the store for little more than a year in the late 1930s, remembers a salesman asking him if he enjoyed his work at the store. "I told him yes, I did, but I was planning to do something else. I was only a teenager. Mr. [Joseph] Kopetsky overheard, and he later told me how disappointed he was in me."

Remembering Lauermans

After a stint in the army during World War II, my father returned to Marinette, and to Lauermans. In 1946 he took the reins from Louis Peters as manager of the cameras, stationery/cards, toys, religious items and gifts, school and office supplies, crockery, Christmas decorations, and gift wrap. People still remember him well.

"Of all the characters at the store," says Frank Lauerman III, "there wasn't a stronger person outside the Lauerman family itself than your dad. Of all the managers, he was probably the most trusted. Newly hired people were often sent to work for him in the crockery department to see if they were any good. F.X. set a standard for his people. Everyone who worked for him loved him."

Judy (Dugan) Hopfensperger agrees. "Mr. Leannah prepared you for what was expected of you in the work world. We should have a Mr. Leannah teaching the young people entering the workforce today."

The young clerks who worked for my father called him "Mr. Leannah," not Francis or F.X., and certainly not by his nickname, "Peasoup." So no one could blame Judy for her

My father, Francis X. Leannah, at his post in the stationery department in the early 1970s.
| *Michael Leannah*

mistake the day a salesman emerged from the second-floor elevator and asked her, "Where will I find Peasoup?" "In the basement in the grocery department," the young clerk replied. The man left, only to return minutes later. "Peasoup isn't in the grocery department," the man said. A coworker of Judy's overheard the man and explained with a good laugh that Peasoup was her boss, Mr. Leannah.

For many, my father was a memorable part of the Lauermans experience. "I don't think your father knew how to walk slowly," says Dorothy Pronold. "He had one speed: *zoom!*" Judy Filbert remembers, "When you'd go in the store, you'd hear Francis's laugh before you'd even see where he was." Gloria Hannon perhaps says it best: "He always acted like you were his favorite person."

"Your father never asked of anyone what he wouldn't do himself," Frank Lauerman III recalls. "He treated everyone the same; it didn't matter who it was. I worked for him for two summers in the wholesale building. One day I was piling stacks of heavy platters, and I got tired. My rear end barely hit the box I was sitting on and—'Lauerman, get off your lazy ass.' He did what he asked you to do, and more, so you didn't mind doing it. He influenced everybody at that store."

Many employed by the Lauermans could not have found work elsewhere. In an era before the words "disability act" passed the lips of any politician, Lauermans seemed to have an instinct for people's needs. When Chuck Boyle, for instance, had an opening in his department, he consulted with area priests for names of people down on their luck. The county government should have thanked Lauermans for their hiring practices; assistance programs weren't necessary for a sizable portion of Marinette's population.

"Anybody who needed a job just had to come to Lauermans," says former employee Fannie Fillinger. "They'd find something for them to do. Handicapped included."

Marinette resident Terry Girard acknowledges the hiring practices of Lauermans and the impact they had on the community. "Today, people who are sixty-five to seventy years old might find jobs at Wal-Mart, but back then they had Lauermans. Some people made fun of Lauermans for having so many elderly people working there, but it was a good thing. Lauermans may not have paid enormous amounts of money, but they kept those people active. And Lauermans offered better working conditions and benefits than Wal-Mart does today."

Aging employees were often allowed to remain with the company in lesser capacities. A changing of the guard at several managerial positions presented itself in the early 1960s. F. J. Lauerman had passed away in 1959, and several of his "lieutenants" (A. J. DeLeers, Jesse Legault, Jack Burke, Art Pfeiffer) had reached retirement age. Meanwhile, a third generation of Lauermans (Chuck Boyle, Frank, Jim, and Henry Lauerman) was waiting to step forward. Because of their longevity and loyalty to the store, the retiring workers deserved careful handling.

DeLeers, for one, continued to appear at his post after retirement. Former employee Mary Falkenberg says that for Lloyd Dufresne, "retirement meant he came into the store only four hours a day."

Chuck Boyle, grandson of Charles Lauerman | *EagleHerald Publishing, Inc.*

Jim Lauerman, grandson of Frank Lauerman | *EagleHerald Publishing, Inc.*

Frank Lauerman III, grandson of Frank Lauerman | *EagleHerald Publishing, Inc.*

Henry Lauerman Jr., grandson of Joseph Lauerman | *EagleHerald Publishing, Inc.*

Sometimes Lauermans carried products well after customer demand dwindled to nothing. If the other stores didn't have the button hook or the radio tube you needed, Lauermans probably had one in a box in the back—or maybe still out on a shelf.

Some employees were more grateful for this practice than even the customers. For more than thirty years Art Nelson was a mainstay in the men's clothing department. Art's specialty was hats. Art *knew* hats. He knew the different styles of hats, how to measure for a hat, everything about hats. "When hats went out of style," says former clerk Chuck Finnessy, "Art Nelson was like a man without a country." In spite of the changing market, Lauermans retained a selection of hats—in the familiar glass display case—into the final years of the store, and occasionally an elderly gentleman would ask for one. You'd have been wise to get out of Art's way when he jumped to life to assist the customer.

A great chemistry and an unusual closeness existed among the workers. Being hired at Lauermans meant more than just getting a job. Employees felt they were part of something special.

What made Tom Plouff stroll down Main Street the day he did when he first encountered Joseph Lauerman looking for hired help? What made my father inquire about a position at the store? Some look back and see their start at Lauermans as a stroke of divine guidance. It wasn't unusual for a person to stop at Lauermans to ask a simple question about job openings and end up staying for half a century.

"When I was a young girl in the 1940s, I applied for a job at Lauermans," says Elsie Mae Bauer. "The man at the desk said he'd let me know if anything opened up. On the stairway I found a wallet on the floor. I took it to the man at the desk. There was sixty dollars in the wallet. It belonged to someone from Upper Michigan. The next day I got a call from the man at the desk. He said because I was so honest he'd find something for me. That was the start of my life at Lauermans, which lasted thirty-nine years."

"We had the nicest employees you could ever want," Frank Lauerman III recalls. "We hired the best people. Quality people. When you hire good people, they make you look good."

Employee pride and loyalty are in evidence even today. On the third Thursday in April, former Lauermans employees gather for a luncheon to visit and reminisce. And members of the Lauerman family are always in attendance.

6

The Top Five

EVERY DEPARTMENT STORE had its specialties: an ornate Santa Claus Village, a holiday parade, a gigantic organ serenading customers as they shopped. People wish they could buy a bag of hot caramel popcorn again from Prange's. They can't suppress a "yummm" at the mention of the Frango mints sold at Marshall Field's. It's the specialty items that many remember most fondly about the department stores of yesterday. And Lauermans provided its fair share, as I came to find out while interviewing people for this book. In this chapter I present for you the five things related to Lauermans that people wanted to talk about the most.

5: The Elevators

The first passenger elevator at Lauermans, installed between 1905 and 1910, was situated in the middle of the store, near the steps to the basement. As small as a closet, the unit was activated by a pull of a cord that jolted it upward before it settled into a smooth ascent. A double-door elevator with six-person capacity soon replaced the original unit and served until the early 1940s, when the familiar twin elevators on the Vine Street side of the building were installed. Floor space on all four levels was sacrificed to accommodate the new elevators; optometrist

Daniel Fast, for instance, lost the second-floor office he had rented from Lauermans.

In our modern world, with trains zipping across the landscape at 200 miles per hour and manned space flights to Mars on the drawing board, it is amusing to note that people were once petrified at the thought of riding in Lauermans' slow-moving elevators. Historian Larry Ebsch says that "riding the elevators from basement to top replaced the thrill of carnival rides."

Some people, afraid of the elevator falling or getting stuck between floors, found the ride more frightening than thrilling. Nervous parents told their children to keep fingers away from the doors. There wasn't much anyone could do to convince such people of the elevator's safety; for them, the stairs provided a less dangerous option. (Some remember the stairs themselves as a thrill. Rita Sadowsky says, "We thought it was wonderful to walk up three flights.")

Dan Ryan, who as a teenager in the late 1930s made doughnuts at the store, states that "the elevator operator doubled as the night watchman. He was the one who let me in at five in the morning so I could get the doughnuts made. I remember him calling out each time the elevator stopped:'First floor! Jewelry! Men's wear! Shoes! Notions!'"

The deep baritone voice of elevator operator Norm Behrendt is recalled by many: "Third floor!" "Second!" "First floor!" He rarely used the word *basement* when the car reached that point, relying instead on:"Bottom!"

Lauermans' attendant-operated elevators continued until the early 1970s, when a retooling turned them into self-service units. But customers from earlier days perhaps can still hear Mardee Parkinson, Joe Osier, or Jake Lindsay calling, "Going up!"

4: Bulk Candy

Though for years candy was sold in Lauermans' basement grocery department, most people today remember the candy counter being positioned in the heavy traffic area in front of the elevators on the first floor. The clerk stood inside the square of glass display cases filled with chocolates, gumdrops, peppermint sticks—every kind of candy a person could want. When a customer called for a half pound of coconut chews or ten cents' worth of chocolate stars, the clerk, using a metal scoop, shoveled a small heap onto the fancy scale, then slid the goodies into a paper bag, nice as you please. (Boxes of wrapped candy and gum, perched on top of the bins, were also available.)

Remembering Lauermans

"I'll always remember the time when I was six or seven, and Charles Lauerman took a little bag and filled it with candy and gave it to me." —*Joyce Stolinberg*

Area resident Ron Nordin says "One of the fondest memories of my childhood is going to Lauermans. All the different kinds of candy in all those bins, and you could buy as much as

Specials in the Candy Section

For Saturday's Selling.

1 lot Gum, 5c pkg. 2 for	**5c**
Salted Peanuts (Spanish) the best per lb.	**8c**
Peanuts, fresh roasted, 10c quality, per lb.	**8c**
Chums and Crackerjacks, the 5c pkg, 2-5c pkgs for	**7c**
Fudge, Assorted, special per lb.	**8c**
Crystal Jelly Slice, per lb.	**8c**
Nawacco Wafer, the 5c pkg., special	**3c**
Waverly Cream Mint Wafers, the 5c pkg., while they last	**2c**
Bon Bons Dish, the 65c pkg., special	**40c**
Fresh 1914 Shelled Walnuts, fancy stock, all halves, no broken, special per ½ lb.	**25c**

Basement.

Lauermans always boasted a good selection of candy, as in this ad from 1915.
| *EagleHerald Publishing, Inc.*

you wanted, a quarter pound, whatever. There was bin after bin after bin. All sorts of candy."

Pity Kathy Kiel, Joan Krukowski, and the other candy department employees who were continually swatting the hands of fellow employees strolling past and helping themselves to scoops of licorice snaps or chocolate-covered peanuts when they thought no one was watching—and even when they knew someone was. It was a losing battle.

3: Listening to Records in the Music Department

In the 1940s three listening booths stood at the back wall of the music department. Patrons were allowed to take a 78 rpm disk inside a booth and give it a spin. No sense in taking a chance on that record by Red Nichols and his Five Pennies—give it a listen first to see if you're going to like it!

Every week the counter in the music department held a new stack of charts put out by Record City of Mequon, Wisconsin, listing the current bestselling records. In the week of July 6, 1970, the Pipkins held the top of the singles chart with "Gimme Dat Ding." Number 1 on the country and western side was "Humphrey the Camel" by Jack Blanchard and Misty Morgan. Shown here are the Top 10 albums of the week. | *Michael Leannah*

The Lauermans tradition of letting customers sample the music before buying continued into the days of 45 rpm records. People today remember the privilege of sliding the disks—with the great big holes in their centers—out of their sleeves and placing them on the spindle of the player on the counter.

Behind the counter, in individual slots, Record City's weekly Top 80 records presided. "Could I try Number 6?" a customer would ask. She'd stand and listen, tapping her foot and scanning the list for what she wanted to hear next. Headphones had been invented—they were available for purchase twenty feet away—but they weren't used for the listening trials. Everyone from gift wrap to linens heard the songs as they were played. And some of the popular songs of the day were far from popular with the employees on the floor. When, for the twenty-fifth time in a single day, strains of "Sugar Sugar" or "Seasons in the Sun" filled the air, it's a good thing the customer couldn't know what the clerks were thinking. Or hear what they were muttering.

2: The Doughnut Machine

A huge fan blew the aroma out to the sidewalk behind the store, drawing people in for a delectable treat. The Downyflake Doughnut Machine stood near the shoe department on the first floor. SEE THEM MADE! read the sign above, and people flocked to do so.

As a teenager in 1938, Dan Ryan operated the doughnut machine. "The ingredients were in barrels and sacks," he remembers. "I'd put them all in the tube and the batter would come out of this big metal spider, dropping eight rings at a time. It was a great spectacle." Ryan's partner was Sam French, another teenager. Ryan recalls, "We had to make new doughnuts

**Downyflake** *HOT* **Donuts**

Best Bet for Breakfast

Top off an all-American breakfast of fruit juice, eggs and coffee with tempting, tasty Donuts. They're made on the spot by the DOWNYFLAKE Donut machine—fresh—hot—delicious—nutritious! Get your box today!

DOUGHNUTS

Plain, Doz. ......18¢
Frosted, Doz. ....23¢

Lauerman's

This 1946 ad featured Lauermans'
"fresh — hot — delicious —
nutritious" doughnuts.
| *EagleHerald Publishing, Inc.*

every hour or so, we sold so many. We had to clean the insides of the machine with a wire brush once a week, on Mondays."

In the 1940s, customers, especially hungry kids, stood and watched as Martha Lindlof ("the doughnut lady"), Edith Parent, or Blanche Patterson operated the machine, sending the rings floating on the hot grease. A little gadget forced the doughnuts to flip over so both sides cooked. More fun than watching the doughnuts being made was seeing the price: twelve cents a dozen in the very early days. Even better than that was pulling a still-warm one out of a bag and eating it.

As a teenager in the 1940s, Verda Kopetsky worked the doughnut machines—she remembers there being two—when the regular workers took vacations. "There was one in each corner of the work space. We would put in the batter, and the machine flipped them out, and they'd go around the whole circle, turn over, and go around again. We'd drop them into large pans of frosting and twist them once and onto a tray. When they dried we could sell them. I think they sold for twenty-five cents a dozen." (That's the same amount the workers at the doughnut machine made per hour.)

1: The Malt Cones

In the 1930s people called them "frosted malted milk cones." Fifty years later, when people referred to them as simply "malt cones" or, less often, "cone malts," the treats were still many people's favorite part of the Lauermans experience.

Frank Lauerman Jr. purchased the "Sweden Machine" that produced the famous malt cones. Operating the machine was quite fussy and labor-intensive. Canisters of malt mixture that weren't completely empty could not be saved for another day, so whatever wasn't used at day's end had to be discarded. For this reason, if a canister was emptied late in the day, a new one was not started, a sure disappointment to late shoppers requesting a cone at 4:30 in the afternoon.

Dan Ryan remembers when the "ice cream machine" first came to Lauermans. "The young man who sold it to Frank Jr. had to teach him and Joe Kopetsky how to use it. You know, the first cone out of each batch was always the best, and I would usually get it. I ate too much of that stuff. Got pimples."

Everyone wants to know what happened to that magical machine. If only it could be found, they think, we could all enjoy those delicious cones once again. "People still ask me what happened to the malt machine," says Jim Lauerman. "And I have no idea. Someone bought it before we went out of business."

Frank Lauerman III says that over the years the store owned two Sweden Machines, both presumably sold and junked. According to Frank, it wouldn't matter if either apparatus existed today. "The machine was nothing special. It was like a washing machine. It had a paddle in the middle shaped like a screw that got very cold and thickened the mix. The machine itself wasn't important. It was the recipe."

And that appears to be lost. The secret ingredients (chocolate, milk, malt powder, and ???) were mixed at Von Heimburg's Marinette Produce dairy, and the mix was delivered to Lauermans in specially marked, four-foot-tall metal tanks. (A single tank, when properly chilled, filled the machine.) Frank III says the dairy "agreed not to sell the mix to anyone else." Alas, Marinette Produce is long out of business, and no Von Heimburgs remain in Marinette to shed light on the recipe.

From time to time the motor in the malt machine broke down, creating a delicate situation with customers threatening to rise up in open rebellion. No crisis at Lauermans caused more shopper dismay. *What? No cones?* The pressure was on as the resident fix-it man, Smokey Johnson, battled with his tools to get the thing up and running again as soon as possible.

Many employees ran that machine over the years, but best remembered is Alfred Kaye, previously employed in the grocery department. Kaye was deaf but could read lips, though regular customers usually placed their orders by means of a show of fingers. In the 1960s they weren't giving Alfred the peace sign, they wanted two malt cones.

In some people's memories those cones were so good, it's a wonder they didn't just sit at the counter and eat them one after another. Area resident George Benoit says, "My military career took me to twenty-one foreign countries. I crossed the ocean seven times. I went all over the world and never found anything like those cones."

Remembering Lauermans

"Every shopping trip ended with a malt cone."
—*Darlene Backman*

"You've got to find that recipe," Bob Nordin told me. "You'll make a million dollars."

Hearing a note of finality in the news of the lost recipe, Ron Nordin was less hopeful than his brother. "So there's no chance of ever tasting them again?"

Apparently not.

7

The Departments, From Top to Bottom

Third Floor: Furniture, floor coverings, draperies, print shop, business office.

Second Floor: Ladies' ready-to-wear, hosiery and lingerie, children's clothing, linens, yard goods, gift wrap, music.

Main Floor: Men's clothing, jewelry, drugs, religious items/ gifts, crockery, cards and stationery, cameras, office and school supplies, shoes, candy, lunch counter.

Basement: Electrical and appliances, paint and wallpaper, sporting goods, hardware, housewares, toys.

THAT'S THE WAY IT WAS during Lauermans' last two decades, but in its long history the store saw many changes in layout. A tobacco counter once had a place in the store. Lamps were separate from furniture. There was a ribbon department. And a team of clerks handled nothing but gloves and neckwear, back in the days when stylish travelers asked for such things as driving gloves and auto scarves.

As customer demand changed, so did the department configuration at Lauermans. Each floor has its own history. Let's go for a ride in the elevator and take a look at what's happening in the different departments. Going up!

To the Third Floor, Please . . .

Like most young boys in the days before World War II, Howard Schleihs loved exploring the gigantic department store called Lauermans. His enthusiasm did not extend, however, to the top floor of the store. "The third floor was forbidding," Schleihs remembers. "Kids had no need for furniture or carpeting, so I rarely went up there. Nothing small was sold up there. It seemed so cavernous and empty, devoid of salespeople or customers. We would take one look from the elevator and head back down."

The top floor of Lauermans may not have been interesting to a kid, but it was hardly empty and devoid of activity. The control center of the store—the business offices—occupied

Lauermans office workers in the early 1950s. Payroll manager Charles Bilodeau is in the foreground; behind him and to his left is Loretta Duhaime. In a row behind Loretta are Helen Shefky, Ann Burke, and Estelle Duhaime. To Helen's right is Florence Cleary, and standing between them is Bernadette Weber. In the far-left background is office manager/comptroller Jesse Legault. | *Virginia Bilodeau*

most of the space on the Main Street side. Much of this area, including the owners' private offices in the far corner above Liberty and Main, was off limits and out of sight to the customers. Weekly managers' meetings took place in F. J. Lauerman's spacious office. Informal meetings with fewer participants were called as needed. Frank Lauerman didn't spend much of the day lingering in his office, however; there was too much to do elsewhere in the store, particularly in the offices just outside his door.

Glen Nordin and Bob Getz were independent auditors hired by Lauermans in the early 1950s to inspect the business's financial records. Nordin remembers the offices at Lauermans. "We had to see that their figures balanced out correctly at the end of the year, make sure nobody shoved any cash in their pocket. I remember Jess LeGault chewing tobacco up there and spitting into a big spittoon while reading the *Wall Street Journal*."

Nordin continues: "I remember working up there in the office one summer and oh, was it hot. No air-conditioning. I was working there at an old desk. I had a necktie on and the varnish came off of that desk—all over my shirt and necktie. There were big windows that they'd open up, but oh, it was hot up there."

When air-conditioning finally came to the office, it wasn't for the comfort of the workers, at least not those of the flesh-and-blood variety. In the late 1970s Mary Falkenberg was sent to Chicago to learn how to run the new Burroughs B-800 computer, a monstrous unit that took up the space of a small room. She recalls, "Everyone envied me up there after that because the computer had to be kept in an air-conditioned environment, so I got to work in the one place where it wasn't so hot."

In the days before computers, charge accounts were processed by office personnel using a card system. When a charge order came through, an office clerk inspected the information

Paying with plastic was an option at Lauermans in the later years. Fewer digits were needed to make up a customer's identification number back then. | *Michael Leannah*

on record and approved the request by hitting a button and punching a hole in the charge ticket.

"What amazed me," says Falkenberg, "was that in the office one person never knew what the next person was doing. They worked with blinders on." As with an assembly line, one worker took care of a single item without knowing the next step in the process. "I wanted to know the whole picture," says Falkenberg, "but most of the others didn't seem to care."

Lauermans' "office boys" had a surprising amount of responsibility. Besides running errands for the big shots (*"Take this roll of quarters to Jim Lauerman." "Go get the morning's receipts from the toy department."*), they did the engraving for the jewelry department, counted checks, helped with the advertising, and at the end of the day went from register to register and read the tills. All this seems like a lot to entrust to teenagers working part-time.

"When I was seventeen or eighteen years old," says Mary Falkenberg, "I had to count the money and lock the safe. I remember wondering, 'Are you nuts? Are you kidding me?' But they were instilling responsibility in young people, many of whom stayed with the store for years and years. There were many ways to steal in that office, and someone once did. When he was caught, Lloyd Dufresne said, 'No, that's our fault. We put that chance in front of him when he wasn't ready for it.'"

One of Falkenberg's daily duties was to go with office manager Ralph Keller at day's end to collect the cash from all of the many departments. "We went from register to register and put the money in a shoe box. We'd return to the office with eight or nine thousand dollars. Was this heartland America or what?"

Elsewhere on the third floor was the grand ballroom called the Blue Room. High school graduation banquets, fashion shows, and other social gatherings took place there. Civic groups such as the Rotary and the Lions Club used the Blue Room for their weekly meetings. (There was also a Gold Room, the former stock room for the jewelry department, located on the second floor of the wholesale building, across Vine Street and connected to the main store by second- and third-floor walkways and a basement-level tunnel. The Gold Room fell into disrepair and was later used for general storage.)

Howard Schleihs, whose grandfather manned the tobacco counter at Lauermans from 1906 until his retirement in 1936, remembers the Blue Room as a "tea room salon, with an upscale air, whose entry credential seemingly catered to the upper-middle-class, middle-aged professional, or widowed female. It didn't hurt if a member of your family had his thirty-five-foot Chris-Craft moored next to one of the Lauerman boats in the Yacht Basin." Henry Lauerman Jr. says the Blue Room was comparable in its day to the Empire Room at the Palmer House Hotel in Chicago. With the velvet wallpaper, the ornate ceiling, and the heavy draperies in various shades of blue, the opulence of the Blue Room was something to behold. Rita Sadowski remembers going to the third floor with her childhood friends "just to watch the rich people eat."

Wedding receptions at a department store? In the days of Lauermans' Blue Room, yes. Manager Joe Kopetsky's daughter Verda was married to Henry Otten on the morning of July 15, 1947, at Our Lady of Lourdes Church. After photographs, the wedding party and fifty guests headed to the Blue Room for a celebratory dinner at noon. "I rode the elevator in my

A gathering in the Blue Room in the 1950s. Henry Lauerman Sr. is at front in suit coat. To his left are Carl Widen, Lloyd Dufresne, Herb Guimond, and Tom Pinder. The woman on the far right is Fae Seefeldt.
| *Jean Eggener*

wedding dress," Verda Otten remembers. (The wedding took place on a Tuesday instead of the preferred Saturday, because most of the church choir worked at Lauermans, many for Verda's father. "I need those people," Kopetsky told his daughter.)

For the store's fortieth anniversary in 1930, a program organized by hardware manager Warren Grace was held in the Blue Room. After a speech by Lauermans' credit manager, A.J. DeLeers, a six-layer cake, three feet square and adorned with forty candles, was cut. According to the local newspaper, "The cake was large enough so that each of the company employees had a liberal slice."

Next door to the Blue Room was the third-floor soda fountain, where a customer or Lauermans employee could take a seat at the counter or at one of the tables to enjoy a bit of refreshment. By the end of the 1950s, the quick-serve lunch counter on the first floor had expanded sufficiently to accommodate all in need of nourishment, and the third-floor lounge was converted into a linoleum display room. The Blue Room eventually became a showroom for the carpeting department.

Lauermans boasted of 100,000 square feet of retail space, roughly a quarter of which was on the third floor—the area that seemed so "cavernous and empty" to the young Howard Schleihs. The furniture did seem to go on forever up there. A remodeling in 1935 brought changes in the positioning of the furniture, allowing for fifty to seventy-five living room suites in suggested settings, twenty-five to thirty bedroom suites, and many pieces of dining room furniture as well.

Warren Heider, longtime employee of the paint department, remembers workers moving long rolls of carpeting into the freight elevator: "They opened the shaft so they could shove in the rolls and take them up to the third floor. It was a big production." The workers lugging that heavy merchandise to the top floor must have wondered why department stores often favored putting the furniture up on top and the lighter items on the first floor. Retailers knew that customers shopping for furniture will go to where the furniture is kept. Not so for someone looking for cards, handkerchiefs, shoelaces, or gloves.

Yes, Lauermans' third floor may have seemed "cavernous and empty." Beds and sofas and chairs and tables need plenty of room. For a child, the place may have indeed been forbidding and frightening. But Howard Schleis's childhood memories aside, many folks remember pleasant aspects of Lauermans' top floor—a warm greeting from Clem Bellemore in the furniture department or a smile from carpeting salesman Wally Rademacher, for instance—and others who worked there.

Let's Make a Stop on the Second Floor . . .

The removal of the grocery department from the store's basement in the early 1960s opened up floor space that allowed for the reorganization of several departments. In the ensuing years the toy department was moved from the second floor to the basement, and stationery, office supplies, and crockery went down one flight to first, swapping space with yard goods and notions. As a result of these moves, other second-floor departments, such as ladies' ready-to-wear and music, had room to expand.

Prior to the renovation, books and magazines (as part of the stationery department) were displayed in a large stand near the freight elevator. Lauermans not only sold books but rented them as well. My family owns a copy of H. G. Wells's *The Fate of Man* with an ink stamp inside the front cover that reads: "Lauerman's Rental Library. This book is also for sale." Above these words is a series of squares numbered one to twenty. None of the squares is marked in any way, so this particular book was bought outright. No one seems to remember how the rental system worked, but the book stands as proof that Lauermans did whatever it took to meet the needs of its customers.

People do remember the elaborate doll display in the second-floor toy department, and the model trains. "When F.X. [Leannah] took over the toys," says Jim Lauerman, "he always had model trains running on great big long tables. At Christmastime, the toy department pushed into the crockery area." The basement toy department of later years is not remembered for train displays—there wasn't room.

Over the years, the second-floor music department was forced into more changes than any of the other departments. Before radios and TVs existed, the big movers in Lauermans' music department were musical instruments—pianos, especially—and sheet music. Phonographs and record players, in all

TUNE-IN THE BIG GAMES!

with a **NEW 1937**

PHILCO

You'll get a new thrill when you listen to the big football broadcasts with a 1937 Philco! Come in . . . see and hear these marvelous values . . . and let us demonstrate!

Free! **"OFFICIAL FOOTBALL FACTS"** *by HolGelfinger*

Valuable 48-page book. Packed full of football history, rules, terms, 1936 schedules, 1935 scores, etc. Get your copy—FREE!

PHILCO 60B $**33**.50

A big-value Baby Grand for American reception. Latest features—fine tone—beautiful modern cabinet.

EASY TERMS!

Lauerman's

LLOYD'S *Department Store*

In my days at the store in the mid-1970s, the music department sold records, stereo systems, TVs, guitars, and radios. The radios were small, encased in plastic, and had AM and FM dials—nothing like the "new" 1937 Philco radio shown here in an ad from September 1936. | *EagleHerald Publishing, Inc.*

their changing forms and styles, also graced the shelves. Some people remember recording booths in which one could cut a song onto a disk.

"My cousin Mary and I took piano lessons during high school from Mrs. Hastings in Menominee," says Joan (Lauerman) Alfredson. "We'd practice for our recitals when the store was closed. They had a room full of pianos. My dad gave us the key to the store, and we practiced together at our own pianos."

The second floor bustled more than the third; there were more departments, and therefore more clerks. Traffic was heavy as customers and employees crisscrossed paths, chatting and laughing. Many of the store's most congenial employees spent their hours on the second floor. The day just seemed brighter when you got a smile from someone like Jean Vedra or Evelyn Barrett. Longtime employee Betty Sladek remembers three women in ladies' ready-to-wear calling themselves "the three little stinkers:" Bea Olsen, Bea Snyder, and Bea McCarthy—Bea O., Bea S., and Bea M.

This 1961 ad directed shoppers to Lauermans' second floor for stockings, "for when you want to be really well groomed." | *EagleHerald Publishing, Inc.*

For those who didn't experience life before "ladies' ready-to-wear," the term is rather puzzling. Was there such a thing as clothes *not* ready to wear? Yes. At the turn of the century most women made—or hired someone to make—much of their families' clothes. After ready-to-wear for women hit the scene in 1915, store's fabric and ribbon departments shrank. (Though Lauermans, in 1917, still advertised: "Washed 98-lb. flour sacks, first quality, most economical at 10 for $1.00.")

Though clerks in all departments freely dispensed help and advice to customers willing to listen, the women in ladies' ready-to-wear perhaps did it best. "I relied on Helen Rademacher in the women's department to help me shop for my wife," says Menominee resident Larry Ebsch. "She knew my wife's colors, her sizes, her tastes."

Remembering Lauermans

"In the 1940s, Dad bought nylons for Mom at Christmastime. He asked for 'a pair that'll wear like iron.' They gave it to him, three pair in a box." —*Darlene Backman*

More than one woman—actually more than three or four—remembers being a self-conscious girl trying on her first brassiere in a Lauermans dressing room, only to be horrified when a well-meaning elderly clerk barged in to ask, "Well, how does it fit?"

Main Floor!

The managers on the first floor had offices in lofts or mezzanines that provided bird's-eye views of the goings-on below. In the store's earliest days, the business office was in a first-floor loft. The loft that became Chuck Boyle's office space above men's clothing was built in 1912 and at the time provided manager Austin M. Wilson additional space for jewelry engraving and other tasks related to his "art goods" and "fancy work" departments. That balcony area was used in the 1940s by tailor Andrew Payant and his wife for doing alterations.

Determining who was who in the history of the men's clothing department is difficult, due to the great number of subdepartments in that area. Chuck Boyle was the manager of the whole department; before him it was Emil Voscamp. Ed Kieff was in charge of men's furnishings (belts, wallets, and so on), and Walter DeVoe was manager of men's underwear and sweaters. Men's work clothes had its own manager, as did men's overalls and gloves. And there was yet another subdepartment

An early photo of the men's clothing department. Without a single clerk on the scene, this photo was probably taken after hours. | *Frank Laverman III*

called "men's goods" that offered hand-kerchiefs, ties, and other accessories.

Howard Schleihs recalls that in the 1940s all of the employees in the men's department were men in their fifties and sixties. Later there were plenty of women and younger workers in the department.

The linen department moved in the 1960s from the first floor to second, but some will always think of that department as the domain of Joseph Kopetsky, manager of several first-floor departments in the '30s, '40s, and '50s.

Joseph Kopetsky, employed at Lauermans from 1925 to 1955 and seen here in 1940, managed several departments. | *EagleHerald Publishing, Inc.*

Kopetsky did much of the hiring for Lauermans in those years. His fluency in Polish, German, and Bohemian came in handy when immigrants entered the store with questions about the merchandise.

Clarence Watkins, head of the sewing machine department, was adept at stitching monograms on handkerchiefs. His

In this undated photo of Lauermans' fabric department, note the overhead basket — part of the Lampson system once used at Lauermans for transferring money and paperwork from departments to cashiers. (For more on the Lampson system, see page 109.) | *Frank Lauerman III*

specialty was taking a person's signature and stitching it perfectly into the fabric.

Frank Lauerman Jr. presided over the jewelry department from the mid-1920s into the 1960s. Monica Barry, later Frank Jr.'s wife, is recalled for her days in the department as well. Both are remembered for their remarkable cordiality, perhaps emulated by Ray Pinkowski, Joe Hutchinson, and others on the main floor with reputations for kindness and grace.

A large, mahogany-paneled telephone booth stood near the Dunlap Square entrance until its removal in the 1950s. The simpler pay phone that replaced it was eventually taken out as well, as it didn't get much use. According to Frank Lauerman III, "People usually just asked a clerk and were allowed to use the phone behind the counter."

Nestled between the school supplies and the shoes was the religious items and gifts department. Boxed rosaries and crucifixes were found inches away from the "gifts," which comprised everything from judge's gavels to incense burners to little plastic boxes with naughty rubber body parts springing out when you opened them.

My father, Francis Leannah, survived for years as manager of the camera department in spite of his proclivity for mispronouncing the word *film* as "fillim." What did knowledgeable customers think when, after purchasing Kodak's latest model, my father hit them with the question: "How much fillim do you want with that?" (In his defense, old movies tell us that in the 1940s, "fillim" was acceptable. Of course, back then *vegetables* had four syllables, and Los Angeles was commonly pronounced "Loss Angle Ease.") Despite his funny way of saying *film*, people trusted Dad's judgment on cameras. Many's the time he was summoned by frantic customers needing emergency assistance with new camera equipment or movie projectors. He made house calls.

A very early photo of the shoe department, first floor | *Menominee Historical Society*

Over in the shoe department, the customers were no less pampered. The kind and patient clerk lovingly removed a customer's shoe before bringing out the ever-present Brannock device, an iron gadget with sliding parts that measures the length and width of a person's foot. The clerk then fitted various styles until a satisfactory pair was found, and the customer left well satisfied. And she got to keep the metal shoe horn.

Several people recall shoe department manager John Victor's sales technique from that era:

Victor: "These shoes are on sale today. A very good bargain. And they fit so well."

Customer: "They seem to be a little too big."

Victor: "Not if I push a little tissue paper into the toe. They really are a good bargain."

Howard Schleihs remembers Lauermans in the World War II years "accommodating my mother's demand for my high-top shoes, dutifully acquired with OPA ration coupons." And some people recall a (thankfully) brief period when the shoe department offered X-rays of customers' feet to help in determining the very best fit.

The lunch counter livened up the east end of the first floor. With a steady stream of shoppers and employees stopping for refreshment, there weren't many lulls in the day over there. Regular customers could count on the waitresses knowing their preferences for extra mayonnaise on their sandwiches and lots of ketchup with the fried potatoes.

"They'd run specials on meals at the lunch counter," recalls Glen Nordin. "The line ran halfway down the block with people waiting to get in. This old guy says to me, 'They've got Swedish meatballs today. The best goddamned meatballs you ever ate.' I can see that guy yet with his big mackinaw on, standing in the cold."

For a number of years my father's office was in the loft above the shoe department, adjacent to the lunch counter. We

LAUERMAN LUNCH
PLEASE PAY WHEN SERVED

SANDWICHES

Baked Ham	40¢
Ham Salad	30¢
Egg Salad	25¢
Tuna Fish	30¢
Lettuce & Tomato	25¢
Liver Sausage	30¢
Cheese	25¢
Peanut Butter	20¢
Peanut Butter & Jelly	25¢
On Toast 5¢ Extra	
Cheese & Crackers	15¢
Toast & Coffee	24¢
Hot Dog	20¢
Chili	25¢

PASTRIES

Doughnut	5¢
Sweet Roll	10¢
Cake	15¢
Pie	20¢
Pie and Cheese	25¢

(over)

LAUERMAN LUNCH
PLEASE PAY WHEN SERVED

SUNDAES

Chocolate	20¢
Pineapple	20¢
Cherry	20¢
Marshmallow	20¢
Strawberry	25¢
Choco-Marshmallow	25¢
Hot Fudge	25¢

SODAS

All Flavors	20¢

MALTS

Malted Milk	25¢
Milk Shake	25¢

FROSTED MALT

Regular	10¢
Large	20¢

(over)

Imagine: A sandwich and a drink, topped off with a frosted malt cone, all for about a half a buck. This lunch counter menu from the mid-1960s promised these and other delights for hungry shoppers. | *Joseph A. Lauerman Jr. Family* at home knew of his fondness for burnt toast, and the lunch counter crew came to know of it too. When the smell of burning bread wafted into the upper air currents, Dad would jump up from his desk, lean over the rail, and shout, "Don't throw that away! I'll be right down!" After a while he didn't have to call to them anymore. They knew. By the time he got down they'd have it buttered for him.

Let's See What's Going on Down in the Basement . . .

In most department stores, the basement was set aside for bargains and liquidation of merchandise. Not so for Lauermans. As customers descended the basement stairs, to their left were appliances, to their right was hardware, and straight ahead, filling the distant half of the basement, lay the grocery department.

Can you see it? The glass bins filled with cookies, the barrels of apples and crackers and peanuts, the meat market over there to the left? Can you smell the bacon hot off the skillet, being offered for customers to sample? There's Charles Lauerman himself, sharing a laugh with a customer as he tallies up her order.

The grocery department flourished from the start due to Charles Lauerman's recognition of a need to accommodate the large number of people in Marinette County who wanted to trade at Lauermans but couldn't regularly pay in cash. In the days before checkbooks and credit cards, bartering was an option, especially in the summer months with farms at peak production. In exchange for chickens, pigs, or potatoes, people were given store vouchers or "due bills" to buy shoes, overalls, and other goods. The trading of produce even led to occasional county fair–style farm shows at the store, with ribbons awarded for the best produce. Charles Lauerman, with assistance from

Farmer's market–style displays like this one on the basement steps in 1918 were common in Lauermans' early days. | *EagleHerald Publishing, Inc.*

Robert Cleary, conducted the bartering, which remained a brisk business into the days of the Great Depression. (Cleary later succeeded Charles Lauerman as grocery manager.)

Just about anything was fair game for trading at Lauermans. The store once burned wood and coal in gigantic furnaces and boilers. Rural customers gained merchandise vouchers in exchange for eight-foot-long logs that were fed to the fire. When the mountainous piles of wood on Vine Street grew too large, newspaper ads featured "slab wood" for sale.

Remembering Lauermans

"Farmers from Sturgeon Bay boarded at my grandmother's house on Friday nights. They sold their things on Saturday morning at the farmer's market near Lauermans. They'd go home having sold all their stuff, but then they were full of stuff they'd bought at Lauermans." —*Lois McLeod*

Old grocery advertisements tell much about the eating habits, lifestyles, and economic conditions of earlier eras. In a 1904 ad, Lauermans offered these specials: "Imperial Drips table syrup—30c per gallon." "Caramel Coin syrup, very fine for the table—40c per gallon." "Cream of Wheat" Minnesota hard wheat flour—100 lbs. for $2.60." "Pure kettle rendered Leaf Lard, none better, just received fresh—9c lb."

In that same year Lauermans held a "Saturday only—Special Market Basket Sale." For one dollar, yours was a basket containing nine bars of Gold Leaf soap, one can of peaches, one pint of pure mustard, one can of salmon, one pound of A. & H. Saleratus (baking soda), a 3.5-pound can of choicest pumpkins, one pound of raisins, two wood coat hangers, and one bar of pure Castile soap. And you were allowed to keep the basket. At one dollar, this was "a clear saving of 54c." They must have wanted to empty the shelves of these items, because the ad made it clear: "In order to get the benefit of these low Grocery Sundry prices, the complete list of goods must be taken."

Innumerable bins full of bulk foods as well as shelves and glass cases loaded with canned and bottled goods awaited thrifty customers in Lauermans' grocery department in the early 1900s. The table at left in the foreground is stacked with boxes of "Kinder Kandy" and "Kokonut Kakes." | *Charles J. Lauerman Family*

In the 1920s Lauermans advertised cookies and crackers included Snow Peak Cakes, Crested Hobbies, Coconut Jumbles, and Coconut Lemon Fingers, all selling for nineteen or twenty cents a pound, sold in bulk from the large windowed cabinets across from the cigar and tobacco counter. In the meat department, veal shoulder roasts and clubhouse steaks sold for twenty-two cents per pound. If that was too high for your budget, pigs' heads went for five cents a pound. Also available were Good Luck Milk—twelve cans for $1.10; Blatz Malt Syrup, hop flavored, light or dark, two cans for a dollar; and "Table Quality" prepared mustard.

Nearly everything was sold in bulk; people who baked in large quantities needed ingredients to work with. Rita Sadowski remembers fifty-pound sacks of flour and sugar delivered to her family's house. "And we sold tons of peanuts in the shells," recalls Frank Lauerman III. "They were very inexpensive and nobody else had them. They were scooped into a bag and weighed on the scale."

Lauermans was the only area grocery to offer delivery. Customers calling before 10 a.m. got their goods the same day; cash-and-carry customers paid slightly lower prices for their items. Friday evening was a popular time for grocery shopping. Families made their selections and then waited for the groceries to be delivered on Saturday morning. Another option was to order by telephone; callers "shopped" with confidence, assured that someone they knew personally would pick the best available items for them.

"My mother would phone the meat and grocery department," says area resident Larry Ebsch. "Mr. Beauparlant was our neighbor in Menominee and a butcher at Lauermans. He would put the order together and drop it off for us when he came home for noon lunch. He handed my mother the slip, she paid him, and he returned it to the department when he went back to work."

At one time Lauermans had twenty-five employees in the meat department alone. Up to eight butchers were kept busy at Lauermans' meat market, which billed itself as "the Sanitary Meat Market" (implying, perhaps, that the others in town were not?). Much of the meat was cooled by ice until electric refrigerating machines were purchased in the late 1940s. An enormous meat locker/freezer stood behind the counter. (This freezer was so big and cumbersome that it remained in place for years after the grocery department ceased to be, serving as a storage closet for the electrical department.) With the deep-freeze unit, Lauermans was able to supply meat for Red 'n Ed's Supper Club, the Wausaukee Club, and other local dining establishments. The restaurants kept quarters of prime beef in Lauermans' deep freezer, to be delivered as needed.

"The butchers used to kill chickens in the basement," recalls Chuck Boyle. "They did it in the fire hole, where the delivery department was later." Turkeys raised by Lauerman relatives from southern Wisconsin were butchered there as well.

Carol Hone Payne remembers her grandmother, Edith Nystrom, working in Lauermans' basement. "She scrubbed floors and washed rags from the meat market and bakery. She washed them on the third floor, in a large room behind the furniture area. She used a wringer washer and hung the wash indoors on long clotheslines."

Mary Ann (Delfosse) Langill worked in the grocery department from 1946 through 1950, taking dictation from Charles Lauerman. "He always called me 'Girly.' He'd call me in and dictate long, long letters. Often they were to the sisters in Chicago, about the girls' camp he founded. My office duties included making sure the invoices matched the receiving slips. The store got a 2 percent discount from the supplier if we paid our bill within ten days, so I had to go over to the warehouse and get those slips and match them up. If I didn't get those papers up to the office in time, I'd hear about it."

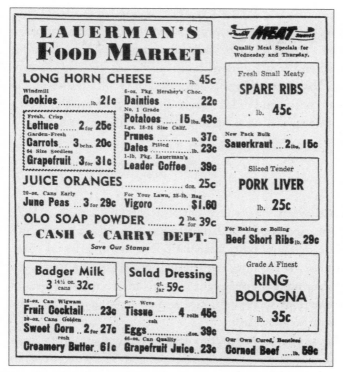

This 1950 ad for the grocery department promoted Lauermans' trading stamp program. (For more about the trading stamps, see page 108.) | *EagleHerald Publishing, Inc.*

Langill remembers Esther King and Violet Loose taking grocery orders by telephone every morning. In the afternoon, Violet moved to the floor as sales clerk, while Esther remained at the phone taking orders. It was Alfred Kaye's job to box orders for delivery. Langill also recalls "young kids" such as John Corry and Chuck Boyle carrying out customers' groceries.

Though Lauermans' grocery department relied on big suppliers such as Carpenter Cook and Cohodas Brothers, the store continued to trade with independent farmers as well. Langill recalls a Menominee grower bringing in flowers and bulbs.

Lauermans' meat department closed in February of 1960. The remainder of the grocery department followed a couple of years later. Yet it lives on in the fond memories of many customers. "I remember standing with my mother as she paid her grocery bill," says Verda Otten. "The man would give me a hot dog if we paid in full and didn't charge. Fresh, right from the cooler. The hot dogs were smoked, so you could eat them uncooked."

From the 1960s forward, essential departments such as toys, paint, sporting goods, and housewares joined appliances and hardware in Lauermans' basement. The boundaries of these departments sometimes overlapped, and disputes flared up. A neighboring manager might inch his merchandise over and steal some floor space, and once a manager staked a claim, he didn't want to give it up.

Longtime employee Jerry Blohm remembers a difference of opinion between Matilda Stromer and Ted Soderberg. In the days of Lauermans' grocery department, bulk cookies and candy were sold from long counters near the bottom of the stairs. Soderberg needed more space for appliances and wanted some of that cookie space. Henry Lauerman Sr. intervened. "Do either of you have a deed to this place?" he asked. Both said no. "Well, I do," he said. He made both of them give a little, and the dispute was settled.

A special breed of clerk was needed for the toy department. Grumpy personalities might get by in other areas, but not in toys. For years Fran Marineau and Ruth Cahill were fixtures there, unflappable as kids charged down the aisles, shooting darts, testing yo-yos, and rolling cars across the floor. Ruth Cahill remembers, "When I went grocery shopping, little kids would say, 'There's the toy lady!'"

Customers' purchases went to the basement packaging department to be wrapped and stored until it was time to head for home. The employees pictured here appear to be up to the task. | *Charles J. Lauerman Family*

Elsewhere in the basement, there once was a small room situated under the Main Street sidewalk (down a narrow row of stairs from the shoe department), in which a man named Frank Chervenka repaired shoes. "Nobody ever saw him," says Frank Lauerman III. "He was in there with all these machines, and he'd put soles and heels on shoes and boots. I remember the smell of the leather. He was like a troll under the bridge. You'd drop 'em off there and pick them up and they were done. He was a fine man." "It was like a little cave in there," adds Chuck Boyle. "Norm Harpt took over after Chervenka retired."

Warren Heider, for years a stalwart member of the paint and wallpaper department, remembers the 1940s when cans of paint were shipped to the store in barrels packed with sawdust. One would suppose that combustible sawdust would not be a welcome addition to the already flammable environment of a paint department, but that wasn't the only thing to worry about in this corner of Lauermans' basement. In the late 1970s Heider

In the store's early days, the paint and wallpaper department was on the top floor along with furniture and carpeting. Later it was relocated to the basement in what used to be the grocery department. Ceilings busy with pipes and wires didn't seem to bother anyone. Note the mops being displayed from within a "Fire Patrol" wagon box, borrowed from the nearby toy department. | *Warren Heider*

was nearly electrocuted while operating the paint mixing machine. He reached overhead to plug in the unit when the voltage surged through him. He credits coworker Steve McBride with saving his life by knocking him clear of the wire.

Heider is among the many recalled for brightening up the basement at Lauermans. Others include Flossie Larson, John Corwin, and Sue Tromblay.

And let's not forget that the ever-helpful maintenance crew had their headquarters in the basement. Their presence at a time of crisis (water spurting from a pipe, smoke rising from an electrical box) was always enormously welcome.

With a store the size of Lauermans, something always needed fixing, and Smokey Johnson, Lenroy Sulk, and the rest were ready for anything. My sister Sue worked at the store as a teenager and was using the women's restroom near the second-floor freight elevator one day when she bumped her brand-new blue cat-eye glasses into the toilet as it was flushing. "I went to Dad, and he said, 'I'll get Smokey.'" Smokey dismantled the plumbing and got those glasses back. "Mom boiled them and everything, but I don't think I ever used them after that," says Sue. What would Smokey say to that?

A leak in the roof, trouble with the phone system, a faulty boiler on a cold winter day, even Sue Leannah's glasses in the plumbing. Those maintenance guys in the basement could fix it all.

Remembering Lauermans

Maintenance man Norm Johnson was always on the go, and because of the twenty or thirty keys he carried on a ring dangling from his belt, you could hear him coming long before he actually appeared. In the 1970s, when TV remote control units were still quite primitive, Johnson's keys worked as well as — or better than — the hand-held remotes. Whenever he had business on the east end of the second floor, Johnson's jangling keys caused the fifteen display TVs to flash on and off. Those working with prospective TV-buyers hoped he would hurry and be on his way. He did, but he'd be back again, with another wave and a smile.

8

Behind the Scenes

IN THE MORNING, a row of tricycles gleamed in the display window next to the entrance at Main and Liberty; in the afternoon, a dozen dolls gazed back at you when you checked again. Someone had been busy when you weren't looking. Many of the doings at Lauermans went unnoticed or were taken for granted. Let's take a look behind the scenes.

Display

Thanks mainly to Lauermans, window shopping was more of a delight in downtown Marinette than it was in cities three times as big. The store presented merchandise to the viewing public in twenty-four plate-glass show windows, eleven feet wide by nine feet tall. Each expansive window was crowned at the top with 570 beveled glass squares. Twelve of the windows faced Main Street, six looked out on Dunlap Square, and the remainder wrapped around the corners at Vine and Liberty Streets.

For more than forty years, Charlie Neumeier was the man responsible for the displays in the windows. Tom Neumeier remembers sitting on a stool and watching his father work in the corner window at Dunlap and Main. Charlie toyed with the sidewalk crowd by putting the wrong shoe on a mannequin's foot. Would they notice?

"Fall Opening" hat display in Lauermans' corner show window, early 1900s | *Charles J. Lauerman Family*

Tom recalls the laughter his response brought when as a child he was asked what his father did for a living: "He putzes with ladies"—the lady mannequins in the display windows at Lauermans. Crowds gathered when Neumeier appeared in the window. They laughed when he feigned embarrassment while adorning a naked mannequin first with a bra, then a slip, and finally a fashionable dress.

"My father always spoke highly of Charlie Neumeier," says Verda Otten, daughter of manager Joseph Kopetsky. "He was talented and artistic." Otten recalls a crowd-pleasing display in the late 1930s featuring a model of the White House made entirely of bars of Ivory soap.

Charlie Neumeier, seen here in 1940, was Lauermans' display manager from the late 1920s through 1970. He was the display manager at the Lloyd Wonder Store in Menominee before taking his post at Lauermans in 1928. | *EagleHerald Publishing, Inc.*

This ad from 1928 offered customers a chance to guess the number of fountain pens laid out in a featured display window. Those in charge at Lauermans were a trusting bunch; the ad says: "In the case of a tie, the person whose answer was received first will be the lucky one, so when sending your answer state date and hour." | *EagleHerald Publishing, Inc.*

Warren Heider calls to mind a Christmas display in a window facing Dunlap Square that included a large mechanical Santa Claus belting out a good, loud "Ho! Ho! Ho!" every thirty seconds or so. Kids loved it, but an annoyed Riverside Avenue resident complained, and Santa was silenced.

Charlie Neumeier was also in charge of the interior decorations for the store, often laboring long hours making Christmas wreaths and other items. My sister Mary Girard recalls Christmas decorations shimmering from floor to ceiling on the pillars in the store. "Those decorations must have gotten old and worn out, because one year they weren't there anymore. But for years they were there, and I just loved them."

After Neumeier's retirement in 1970, Ray Pinkowski inherited the task of decorating the display windows. Dorothy Hatch and Barb Palzewitz are also remembered for their display skills at Lauermans. When it came time to purchase the windows back in 1904, the Lauerman brothers didn't start pinching any pennies. The windows themselves are a marvel, remarkably beautiful still today.

The store's anniversary was always celebrated in a big way. There seemed to be no shortage of ideas on how to use the celebration day to draw in the customers, and often the display specialists were included in those brainstorming sessions. In 1940, to mark the store's golden anniversary, the large Lauermans sign was taken off the roof to make way for a three-tiered, three-dimensional cake facsimile that jutted out over the sidewalk on Dunlap Avenue in a way that made the cake appear to run directly through the store. The fifty-foot-tall cake was festooned with gold stars, candles, and neon lights.

Delivery

From their earliest days in business, the Lauermans used a horse-and-wagon delivery system. It was not a simple operation. The horses needed to be stabled, fed, and groomed, and harness makers and blacksmiths were kept busy. The horses were quartered in a barn a few blocks from the store, near the Marinette County Courthouse. Delivery foreman John Arndt led the horses to their duties at the store each morning. Lauermans did not completely phase out the use of horses until 1950. "At first we had horses only, of course," says longtime office manager Lloyd Dufresne. "Then we got one truck, then another, and gradually more."

Former employee Martha Mogensen recalls the horse-drawn delivery vehicles from her childhood: "They delivered

Lauermans' horse-drawn delivery wagon. In this undated photo, the wholesale building can be seen in the background at left. | *Frank Lauerman III*

This undated photo of a Lauermans delivery truck was taken in the same area near the wholesale building. Note the change in the pavement. | *Frank Lauerman III*

with wagons and sleighs in the alley behind our house. The sleighs were lower to the ground than the wagons, and we kids would jump on the runners and hang on and take a ride. Mr. Gray was the driver. He didn't want us there, of course."

A contentious dispute arose in the early 1960s when the state of Michigan attempted to force Lauermans to impose its state tax on goods sold to Michigan residents. After Lauermans' trucks were intercepted and held in Michigan, a lawsuit was filed and a settlement was reached. If a Wisconsin business's own trucks were not used to make its deliveries, Michigan's tax laws could not be enforced. This ruling led to the sale of the Lauermans delivery system to Glen Larson, whose father, Axel Larson, had managed Lauermans' delivery service for decades. Legally the Larsons now owned the service, even though the Lauerman name was emblazoned on the trucks.

Remembering Lauermans

"My mother would call the store in the morning before ten o'clock and place her order. They delivered it by noon. If she forgot something, she'd call back, and they had an afternoon delivery. Two deliveries a day."
—*Joan Alfredson*

The changing of the guard. What did those horses think of the motorized trucks encroaching on their territory? | *Frank Lauerman III*

When Lauermans discontinued its grocery department in the early 1960s, other grocers in the area (A&P, Krambo's, Red Owl, Malmstadt's, and others) gave a sigh of relief. Only Lauermans, with a delivery system for furniture and appliances already in place, could afford to offer free delivery of groceries.

Remembering Lauermans

Like so many of the earlier niceties, delivery of small items was discontinued in the later years—which some people couldn't bring themselves to accept.

"In 1990, Lauermans had a store in the mall in Marinette," says Jim Lauerman. "A guy from Menominee called and asked, 'Do you have any union suits?' We had some, left over from World War I or something. He said, 'How much are they?' I said, 'Ten bucks.' He said, 'Send me two pair.' I said, 'Sir, we don't deliver.' 'What do you mean, you don't deliver?' I said, 'Well, sir, we haven't delivered in years.' 'Well, I always ordered from Lauermans and they delivered it the next day or that same day.' I said, 'Well, when you come over to the mall sometime they'll be here.' He said, 'I haven't crossed the bridge in twenty-five years.' He never came for those union suits."

Security

In the early days of Lauermans, shotgun-toting night watchmen patrolled the aisles of the store and warehouse, and in the 1930s an employee armed with a shotgun stood guard as the money was counted in the office every evening. It was rare for the store to summon the police, even after the commission of a crime. Occasionally employees were caught filching money, or shoplifters were apprehended; Lauermans preferred to handle such matters from within. "Lauermans never prosecuted anybody," says former employee Betty Sladek. "Shoplifters were usually just escorted from the store."

Sladek also remembers a time when butter was disappearing from the grocery department. "They found an employee smuggling butter out of the store by wrapping it in the tops of her stockings. They called her 'Butterlegs' after that." But she remained employed.

There wasn't a need for a formal security detail until the 1960s, when a number of employee thefts led to the hiring of former Marinette police officer Vic Thedick as store security officer. "Just his presence put an end to a lot of the trouble," says Frank Lauerman III. "He went around and just asked questions occasionally, and that was enough of an intimidating factor."

The security detail at Lauermans may have had a touch of Mayberry USA about it. "Vic Thedick's call number on the P.A. was five-oh," says former employee John Garon with a smile. "Everybody knew who five-oh was. Even the criminals."

Remembering Lauermans

Henry Lauerman Jr. recalls giving chase after being informed that a thief had run out of the store with an expensive guitar. By the time Henry spied the music-loving teenager heading over the Interstate Bridge, the kid was fifty yards ahead of him. When Henry ran, the kid ran. When Henry stopped, the kid stopped. At last, the thief flagged down a friend in a car and off they drove. A passing motorist witnessed the scene and offered to assist Henry. They raced after the teenagers, but lost them in the maze of Menominee streets, after which the "Good Samaritan" drove Henry back to the store. Perhaps the first song the kid played on the pilfered guitar was Chuck Berry's "You Can't Catch Me."

Gift Wrap

On the second floor, in the corner at Main and Liberty Streets, was a room that served as a lounge, with seats along the walls and large windows overlooking the street. Also in that room, scissors-wielding artists such as Erma Madsen and Margaret Retlick worked their magic at the gift-wrapping counter.

"I remember standing in awe at the gift wrap department, watching Sue Leannah wrap gifts," says former Menominee resident Marianne (Hoffman) Conlan. "She was magnificent. We didn't usually have our purchases wrapped, only the things we bought for our mother. We didn't want her to see us bringing her presents home in a bag."

My sister Sue (Leannah) McAllister remembers those days well. "Gift wrapping was free, unless you wanted special paper. Dad was the manager of the gift wrap department, and he taught me how to tie a bow on my hand. That's how I practiced until I got it right. He always said, 'If they can buy it here at Lauermans, we can wrap it.' I remember someone came in with an ironing board, and they wanted it wrapped. An ironing board! I went to Dad and told him I wasn't sure how to do it. He said, 'You'll find a way.' And I guess I did."

Trading Stamps

Lauermans' trading stamp program grew out of a problem: some of the cash wasn't making its way into the drawers. A dishonest clerk would charge a customer 68 cents and put it down on the slip as 27 cents, pocketing the difference.

Frank Lauerman III claims his grandfather, Frank Sr., had to come up with something to correct the problem, and the trading stamp system was born. "He worked out a scheme where you [the customer] would get 2 percent cash back, which they figured was the cost of keeping the clerks honest. So everybody who rang up a cash sale took that ticket and went over to the stamp window and got stamps. Customers started watching their receipts more carefully." An ad in the *Daily Eagle-Star* of April 19, 1905, proclaimed: "Stamps are free with each and

No S&H Green Stamps here. Lauermans had their own trading stamps.
| *Michael Leannah*

every cash purchase of 10c or over, and they are tendered to customers whether they are asked for or not."

A cashier sat in a small cubicle at the top of the stairs leading to the basement, making change, taking customers' inquiries, but mainly issuing stamps after presentation of receipts. There were twenty pages to a stamp booklet, with fifty stamps fitting on each page. Customers received two dollars for a completed book. Completed stamp booklets were cashed in at the office on the third floor.

"If you paid your charge account bill between the first and the tenth of the month, you'd get extra stamps," remembers Jean Eggener, former cashier in the main office. "You wouldn't believe the people who'd come. We were so busy. Today they'd laugh at an offer like that."

The Public-Address System

Before the installation of the public-address system in 1960, Lauermans relied on office boys to run with messages and invoices from one department to another. In the days before cash registers, the Lampson system—a network of baskets running along ceiling wires and upward through a hole to the next floor—delivered money and paperwork from department to cashier and back. Managers communicated with each other by telephone. The office workers depended on a dumbwaiter for delivery of cash and receipts from one floor to another. (The dumbwaiter was encased in a hollow pillar, out of sight of the customers. To send something to another department, employees pulled ropes to lift or lower the box and then used a buzzer to alert the recipient at the desired floor.)

The P.A. system first served to aid communication between the main store and the warehouse but soon operated as systems do today, making announcements for employees and customers and later providing background music. The familiar voices of the women on the store's P.A. system kept both customer and clerk entertained—often unwittingly. Their flubs and missteps added to the charm of the store.

Names were often garbled in humorous fashion, and who could blame the poor P.A. announcers? Some of those northeastern Wisconsin names were tough: Krzeminski, Modschiedler, Palzewitz, Hopfensperger. Legend has it that on one afternoon, "Jim Van Hemelryk" was mispronounced seven different ways. (It may have been a problem with the sound system and not a mistake of the tongue when Blanche Bilodeau referred to Bruce Leannah as "Boots" Leannah. People who were there that day still call him that once in a while.)

Customers couldn't have been pleased with some of the frank announcements, such as, "Would the lady who just purchased the panty pants please return to the lingerie department?"

And the P.A. announcers never said anything just once. "Joe Jones, please return to the sporting goods. Joe Jones, please return to the sporting goods." Certain individuals had code numbers by which they were summoned. "Six-two, six-two," meant Francis Leannah was to call the office. In the 1970s, *Mary Hartman, Mary Hartman* was a popular prime-time soap opera spoof. One dull afternoon, the normally inculpable Mary Falkenberg—after getting clearance that none of the Lauerman brass was in the building—screwed together her courage and called on the P.A. for "Mary Hartman! Mary Hartman!" Anything to amuse the troops.

In another well-remembered P.A. incident, Jerry Haines was busy with a customer at the sporting goods counter and chose not to respond to the operator's call of "Three-twelve, three-twelve." When she called again a minute later, people throughout the store sensed the impatience in her voice. She knew Haines was there in the sporting goods department, ignoring her calls. After her third attempt failed to draw a response, she tossed aside the number code and gave him a loud: "Jerry Haines, pick up that receiver!" You just don't hear those kinds of things in stores anymore.

The P.A. operators also worked the telephone switchboard. People calling Lauermans might imagine the operator with her finger on the pulse of the entire operation. In reality, the women at the controls of the switchboard (Blanche Bilodeau, Mary Falkenberg, Catherine Kehoe, and others) didn't see much of anything. Their quarters were a cramped station nestled among several office cubicles, removed not only from any activity but from virtually any signs of life.

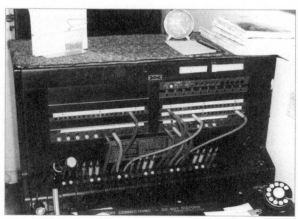

The office switchboard was cutting-edge technology in its day. The one red light indicated an incoming call for F. J. Lauerman.
| Jerry Haines

Lauermans' Wholesale Division

When the big store opened in 1904, Lauermans had warehouses on Main Street, Pierce Avenue, and elsewhere in Marinette. The large building adjacent to the store, just across Vine Street—the building that later became *the* warehouse—was initially the Lauermans' wholesale building. (Actually, three buildings were pieced together to make one; the different architectural styles are evident yet today.)

Lauermans' wholesale division was run as a separate business, though affiliated with the main operation. Small-town independent retailers in northern Wisconsin, Upper Michigan, Door County, and elsewhere relied on Lauermans' wholesale for their merchandise. The wholesale operation made mail-order purchases possible for distant customers as well.

The wholesale division and the retail store were separate operations; employees stayed on their respective sides of the

Proud workers stand on Dunlap Avenue in front of the Lauerman wholesale building in this undated photograph. | *Frank Lauerman III*

street and rarely interacted. Buying in great quantities, however, guaranteed a better price for customers. If the managers in the men's department felt they could sell ten suit coats of a particular kind, the store bought a hundred of them, at a reduced price. Ten coats went to the store and ninety to the wholesale, where they were made available to other stores or to mail-order customers. A team of salespeople serviced the small general-merchandise stores scattered across the state and beyond. When national chains drove the smaller stores out of business, the dominoes fell, and in 1960 Lauermans discontinued its wholesale division.

The Lauerman wholesale building and the Marinette Post Office shared the block bounded by Dunlap Avenue and Vine, Liberty, and Stephenson Streets. In the late 1950s, a new post office was constructed on Maple Avenue. After the old building was razed, Lauermans purchased the land for its parking lot. The wholesale building remains standing today, connected to the store building by a basement tunnel and second- and third-story viaducts over Vine Street.

The Marinette Post Office building was razed in the late 1950s, and the area became the parking lot for Lauermans' store. The wholesale building is in the background on the left, and the department store can be seen in back at right. Note the water tower on top of the store. | *Frank Lauerman III*

The Warehouse

Each department at Lauermans had a worker or two assigned to the warehouse. Their primary duties were to unload and organize incoming shipments and respond to calls for new items to be brought to the sales floor.

By the 1970s, Lauermans' wholesale division was but a fading memory. Young workers wondered why some of the older ones referred to the building occasionally as "the wholesale." By then most everybody called that building "the warehouse." And what a place that warehouse was.

When shipments came in by truck, the merchandise was taken in at the warehouse loading dock and moved into place on one of the four floors. The flow was continuous: as televisions and typewriters and sofas and wheelbarrows were sold on the retail side, boxes and crates were wheeled over the viaduct or through the tunnel from the warehouse.

The interior of the wholesale in the early 1900s. Years later, after the building took on a new identity as the store's warehouse, these same shelves were stocked with miscellaneous merchandise.
| *Charles J. Lauerman Family*

Remembering Lauermans

Henry Lauerman Jr. tells of an employee wheeling a grandfather clock over the second-floor viaduct and knocking off a ceiling sprinkler head, thereby starting a flood. Lenroy Sulk, being the only one with knowledge of the correct valves, was summoned, but not in time to prevent extensive spillage through the floor, down into an open convertible parked below on Vine Street. By the time they stopped the flow, the car was nearly filled to the brim. "Thank you for shopping at Lauermans."

When a manager sent you across the street to get something, you'd leave the brightly lit and noisy environs of the store and enter the dark and spooky world of the warehouse. Stacks of boxes lined your path. The floors creaked beneath your feet. Bare lightbulbs hanging from the rafters cast shadows every which way. The echo of someone's shout in the basement reverberated up the elevator shaft to where you were on the second or third floor. You felt like you were the only one in that whole big building, and sometimes you were. If you tripped and broke your ankle, or if a box fell on your head, would anybody ever find you?

The warehouse certainly held its mysteries. While working there as a teenager in the 1970s, I discovered a secret stairway, dusty and dark, leading from the second floor to the sidewalk on Dunlap Avenue, the door at the street boarded up and nailed shut.

With a store the size of Lauermans, excess goods are bound to accumulate in a warehouse. It was generally understood that if merchandise failed to sell and didn't move even at the yearly sidewalk sale, it was stored somewhere in the vast, cavernous warehouse. This idea gained credibility whenever an employee was sent over there to find a specific item and got lost in a long, tedious rummage through all the assorted stuff gathering dust. Here and there, in crannies and corners, museum-quality items sat on forgotten shelves.

"That warehouse was full of stuff," says Jim Lauerman. "For a play at Catholic Central High School, the costume people needed some old-fashioned spats. They tried to order some. Couldn't find them anywhere. They asked at Lauermans, and we found some in the warehouse."

"I once found six pairs of very old skis tucked up in the rafters in the warehouse," remembers former employee Bob Kiefer. "Henry [Lauerman Jr.] let me have them for six dollars. They were old-fashioned skis, very unusual. I used a band saw and cut them down to size. I ended up with six nice sets of skis."

Being assigned to warehouse duty had its drawbacks, however. Some of the surprises found over there were far from pleasant.

"When I started at Lauermans," says Elsie Mae Bauer, "I worked in the handkerchief department at forty-five cents an hour. Because I was new, they sent me to get stock in that spooky warehouse. I didn't like going over there by myself. That warehouse was dirty, dusty, dungeon-y. No one ever cleaned it up. You'd take stuff from a shelf and dust went right in your face all the time."

The upper floors may have been "spooky" to some extent, but the warehouse basement took the prize for being fearsome and forbidding. While Lauermans' basement retail area was spacious and pleasant, the warehouse was a different story. Former employee Dave Remington recalls the underground tunnel to the warehouse as "kind of dark and gloomy and catacomb-like."

In the days of the grocery, trainloads of sugar, flour, and grain came in to the warehouse building regularly. These bulk foods were weighed, packed into cloth bags, and sold in the retail area. The foodstuff in the basement warehouse led to stories—true or false—of rats and other unpleasant creatures

The basement tunnel entrance to the wholesale/warehouse building. | *Jerry Haines*

lurking in the dark recesses. It was hard to block out those stories as you tramped over there to get that box of paintbrushes or those lightbulbs for the boss . . .

"There was a night watchman who used to walk around the warehouse with a shotgun," claims Jerry Blohm. "He was always scared to death. There'd be rats walking around on the pipes, running around down there because we had seed and all that stuff. Cats were released in the warehouse to cut down the rat population."

Let's offset that horrible image of the warehouse with a cheerier memory from Verda Otten, daughter of manager Joe Kopetsky:

> If Dad had to go to the store to stock merchandise at night, I'd go with him once in a while. He'd lift me up so I could turn on the ceiling lights by pulling the long strings. Then I'd sit at his desk and draw pictures while he worked. If

the janitor from the warehouse came over, he let me take the flashlight and I'd go with him to all the floors of the warehouse to check everything. He had to punch a clock over there to prove that he had gone through that area. He was checking for burglars, but mostly for signs of fire. Fires could start quickly. He made several trips each night. By the time I got back, Dad was ready to go home again.

Otten says she wasn't the least bit afraid of going into the warehouse. Could it be that the skittish night watchman felt safer with a four-year-old girl helping him make the rounds?

Buying Trips to Chicago

From the earliest days of the store until late in his long life, Frank Lauerman Sr.—or, rarely, someone in his place—traveled to Chicago once a week to buy merchandise for Lauermans. He left on the 10:37 train on Sunday night and had a standing reservation for Monday night at the Palmer House hotel in downtown Chicago. The jobbers, or wholesalers, whom F. J. Lauerman commonly dealt with in Chicago included Sam Bass, the House of Kerman, Israel Silverman, and Marshall and Harold Nachbar. These wholesalers dealt with a wide array of closeout merchandise, much of it of the finest quality.

In time others came to earn the trust of Frank Lauerman and were allowed to do some of the buying. My father, Francis Leannah, learned from F. J. Lauerman himself how to strike a proper deal. The third generation of Lauermans (Frank III, Henry, Jim, Chuck Boyle) learned from their grandfather and from men like my father.

"F. X. Leannah knew how to do it," says Frank Lauerman III. "He'd buy paper products or dishes in Chicago for, say, eight cents. They were to sell for eleven cents, but if other stores didn't have it, or if they sold it for seventeen cents, he'd sell for fourteen.

Always had a better price. Your dad was a whiz at that kind of stuff. He bought things thirty for a penny, packaged them, and sold them two for a nickel. He would come back from Chicago with tons of notebooks and things, and I'd say to him, 'What are we going to do with all of that?' He'd say, 'Watch.'"

"This is the way it was," Jim Lauerman explains. "We'd go to Maxwell Street in Chicago. One of the jobbers would say, 'I've got ten thousand typewriters. Brand new, still in boxes.' One guy says, 'I'll take five hundred.' Another says, 'I'll take one hundred.' Fifteen minutes later, all ten thousand were gone. It was just written down. 'Five hundred to F. X. Leannah at Lauerman Brothers.' After World War II, your dad went to the auctions down there and he got to know all those people. We were there with him once, and your dad said to me and Frank and Charlie and Henry, 'You guys stay back here and don't move. Don't raise your hand, don't sneeze, don't say anything. Just watch.' The auctioneer was at the top of a ladder up on the platform conducting the sale. Every few seconds he'd yell, 'Sold! Sold L.B.!' That was Lauerman Brothers. I heard a guy say, 'Who the hell is L.B. doing all this buying?' After a while I said to the fellows, 'What's Peasoup [my father's nickname] doing under that ladder?' All of a sudden I see him reach up and pull the guy's pants leg. And then: 'Sold! L.B.!' It really was fun watching your dad operate."

"I went to Chicago on a buying trip with my father and your father when I was sixteen," Frank Lauerman III recalls. "I remember the dealers: Sam Bass and the House of Kerman. When the jobbers approached us, my father pointed to F.X. and told them, 'This is the man you want to talk to.' I watched your father as he listened to their sales pitches. I remember him saying 'Bullshit' over and over."

"Your dad would only pay so much," says Jim Lauerman. "He'd look at the glassware and tell them, 'Ten cents apiece.' And he'd get the price."

"I was with my grandfather and your dad on a buying trip to Chicago," says Frank Lauerman III. "Sam Bass had fifteen hundred plaster altars with lightbulbs inside and candle holders on the outside. Your father said, 'We could sell those.' My grandfather said, 'Do you really think people will buy them?' F.X. said, 'Oh, yeah.' They tried to make a deal to buy three hundred of them. Bass said they had to buy the whole lot, so the deal was off. Nobody ultimately bid on them, so Bass made another offer. 'We can't use that many,' he was told. Bass said, 'Give me twenty-five cents apiece for them. I've got to get rid of them.' On the train later, F.X. said, 'I can sell half of them for ten times our cost, and the rest we can throw away.' But they sold them all. Every last one of them. I don't know who'd buy them, but they did."

The bargains made on the buying trips to Chicago allowed for Lauermans to keep its shelves stocked with goods that kept customers satisfied and the company's coffers full.

"During times when things were so hard," Verda Otten remembers, "Father went to the warehouses in Chicago and bought bolts of fabric that were damaged in some way. He got them very cheap. He brought the material home, and we made these little woolen babushkas for the kids at school. We cut all these triangle pieces, and Mother and I sat and listened to the radio at night and put crocheted fringes on the edges of the scarves. Father sold those for twenty-five cents or fifty cents. With about ten of those he made the price of a bolt of fabric. The babushkas actually became a fad. It was cold in Marinette in the wintertime. Everybody wanted those scarves to wear to school."

Joseph Kopetsky's colleagues questioned his purchase of a great number of mesh horse blankets, made to keep the flies off the animals. "He cut them into dish cloths for kitchen use," says Otten. "They sold for a nickel or a dime apiece. They worked beautifully."

Sometimes merchandise purchased in Chicago included items slightly or not-so-slightly damaged by fire. "They'd come back from those trips to Chicago," recalls Elsie Mae Bauer, "with boxes of stuff we thought belonged in the garbage. Fire-damaged stuff that was filthy. We had to clean it up and try to sell it." Ruth Cahill says, "We'd clean up that fire-damaged stuff in the Gold Room in the warehouse. We had to run fans in order to breathe."

In the beginning, the store was a simple operation and everything was out in the open. But with growth came complexity—it took many moving parts to keep the Lauerman machine in motion. Much of the day-to-day business was conducted behind the scenes. When a Marinette doorbell rang and a Lauermans deliveryman stood with a package, the lady of the residence accepted the delivery and proceeded with her day. She gave no further thought to the window display that had attracted her attention in the first place. She'd probably forgotten the conversation she'd had with the polite woman on the telephone when she placed her order. She didn't think to ask how Lauermans came to find the charming item or how it became gift wrapped so nicely, or who had fed the horse that pulled the delivery wagon to her door.

She didn't know what happened behind the scenes at Lauermans. Few customers did. But what went on beneath the surface there was expertly coordinated, allowing the business to function like a well-oiled machine. A machine that cranked out customer satisfaction on a daily basis.

9

The Greater Community

THE LAUERMAN INFLUENCE was not confined to the buildings on Dunlap Avenue. Just as a tide lifts all boats, Lauermans' booming business lifted all of downtown Marinette and the surrounding region. Through the years, Lauermans—the family and the business enterprises—affected the community in profound ways. What would Marinette have been without Lauermans? It's hard to imagine.

Friday Nights in Marinette

For many years, Friday night was *the* night in downtown Marinette. That was the one night of the week when the stores stayed open until 9 p.m. (In the early days, stores had evening hours on Saturdays; later it was Thursdays.) Lauermans' employees commonly went home and dressed up for the evening shift. People today recall the Friday night bustle as being almost magical.

"On Friday night, you saw *everybody*," says Jim Lauerman.

"Man, that was a scramble on Friday night," adds former employee Elsie Mae Bauer. "It was like a can of worms, people

Night view of Dunlap Square from Hall Avenue, circa 1930. For many, the installation of electric street lights sparked an interest in shopping after dark. (In the foreground at left is Scheldt and Samuelson Shoes, later Goodfellow's tavern, soda fountain, and variety store.) | *Bob and Eva Kiefer*

all over the place. Nowadays, the stores are open every night, all night long. It's no fun anymore."

On Friday nights—and at no other time—Marinette police officers were needed to direct traffic at Pierce Avenue and Main Street. The sidewalks were crowded with people bumping and jostling.

Frank Lauerman III remembers farmers coming into the store on Friday nights after working in their fields all day. "They stood at the back door by the big radiator, with frozen cow manure on their boots and clothes. As they warmed up, the place started to smell like a barnyard."

Speaking of Friday night fragrances, Marianne (Hoffman) Conlan says, "I remember going to Lauermans on Friday nights to do our grocery shopping. The aroma of ground coffee filled the basement. I remember wishing and hoping to have enough money to go up for a malt cone at the lunch counter."

When the Train Came In

A curious fact persisted through the years: towns twice the size of Marinette couldn't brag of a store half the size of Lauermans. How could a city the size of Marinette sustain such a large enterprise? What people may forget is that Lauermans served a large geographic area stretching a good distance across northern Wisconsin and into the far reaches of Michigan's Upper Peninsula. The store was seen by many as a destination of great significance, a beacon on the hill to farmer and villager alike. A trip to Marinette was an event, something one looked forward to, planned for, saved for. It was an *experience*.

Margaret Swanson remembers bouncing in the backseat of her family's Model T as they rode to Marinette from Crivitz: "I think it took as long to get to Marinette then as it does now to get from Crivitz to Milwaukee." The reward for all their efforts? Entering the doors of the magnificent Lauermans store.

People came by car and bus, and many arrived daily by train. Marinette had two train depots, a stone's throw from each other, off Hall Avenue near Hattie Street. Trains running from Chicago to Upper Michigan made stops at the Chicago-Northwestern depot, while the Milwaukee Road building served trains running to Madison and points west. (One hundred and one years after the beautiful Milwaukee Road depot was built in 1903, Frank Lauerman III saved it from demolition by financing the building's move one block north to its current site.)

A Milwaukee Road spur extended from Marinette to Ellis Junction (now Crivitz), Wausaukee, and Iron Mountain. Lauermans customers from those towns frequently came by train to shop in Marinette. Though some people from the county remember riding into town in a little car pulled at the end of a freight train, most came in the passenger train that ran to the city each day. Frank Lauerman III remembers,

People got on the train at 8 a.m. and arrived at the depot in Marinette at 10. My dad and I would stand at Dunlap Square and look at the people coming like an army of ants, hundreds of people, coming down Hall Avenue. They'd shop on the way to Lauermans [at Goldberg's, Brooks Drugs, Ruth Smith's Confectionary, J. C. Penney, The Arrow Store]. We couldn't wait for them to get to us. They'd arrive loaded down with packages, so we started a storage service. We had a whole department just for holding merchandise. Customers were given a little leather strap attached to a brass ring to identify their belongings. We packed their stuff and brought their purchases to the depot before they left for home at three o'clock. That system lasted for maybe five or ten years.

No stores provided paper bags back then. Twine was used to wrap purchases in brown paper. Handles were sometimes made by running brass wire through pieces of wooden dowel; these could be hooked to heavy packages for ease in carrying. Many customers, not just those from distant parts of Marinette County, shopped all day and picked up their bags at day's end from the transfer department. And Lauermans provided a wagon ride back to the depot for those traveling by train.

Christmas at Lauermans

For countless residents of northeastern Wisconsin and a large chunk of Upper Michigan, it wasn't the Christmas season until they visited Lauermans. Shirley Nordin lived in Stephenson, Michigan, as a girl and recalls, "When I was in second grade, our class rode the train down to Marinette. We saw Santa Claus in one of the back rooms at Lauermans. The walls were all velvety and Santa was there with a gift and a treat for us. It

Notice from the *Daily Eagle-Star*, December 1906. Let's hope the children weren't greatly disturbed by the lyrics in the upper right corner reading, "Toyland, Toyland, little girl and boyland. Once you pass its portals, you can ne'er return again." | *EagleHerald Publishing, Inc.*

must have been on the second floor, because I remember taking the elevator. A school bus later picked us up and brought us back home."

According to Howard Emich's history of Marinette, *Menominee River Memories*, John Farnsworth, the great-grandson of "Queen" Marinette, took time off from his regular jobs as lumber camp cook and hunting and fishing guide to serve as Santa Claus at Lauermans. Since he died in 1944, he must have worked at the store in the 1930s or earlier. Others employed by Lauermans for the role of Santa Claus include Wilbur Shoemaker, Gene Groleau, and Bob Harbick.

In the early 1950s, Lauermans sponsored a daily "Letters to Santa" segment at holiday time on radio station WMAM. Bill Liegeois, in his first broadcasting assignment for the radio station, played the part of Santa Claus. Liegeois stayed with WMAM for decades and is remembered primarily as the announcer for local high school football and basketball games.

Many northeastern Wisconsin natives have memories of visiting Santa Claus at Lauermans. "When Christmas rolled around," says Larry Ebsch, "we took our two boys to the basement to see Santa, played for years by Gene Groleau. We mentioned the kids' names out loud and, of course, Santa welcomed the kids to his lap. They were stunned that he knew their names and remembered them each year."

Early in the store's existence, the office was in a loft on the first floor. In this undated photo, Santa Claus visits with a young customer directly above the cashier. | *EagleHerald Publishing, Inc.*

One of the store Santa Clauses is not so fondly remembered for issuing a lackadaisically lukewarm "Ho Ho Ho" every ten seconds all day long, whether kids were present or not. By the end of their shifts, those who worked within earshot knew what Chinese water torture was like.

Some people's memories of Lauermans are embedded forever, especially the ones involving Christmas. Bonnie Haines remembers at Christmastime in the 1970s leaving her regular post at the switchboard to be the voice of the talking Christmas tree near the elevators on the second floor. A wire ran from Bonnie's hiding place in a cardboard box near the freight elevator to a speaker hidden in the branches of the tree. Through a peep hole, Bonnie saw when children passed, and that's when the magical tree started to talk. "Is Santa coming to your house?" "Have you been good this year?" "What do you want for Christmas?" The tree bowled over unsuspecting adults as well: "Have you gotten your wife a present yet?"

Remembering Lauermans

"At Christmastime, Lauermans was the place to go, with all those toy trains running on the second floor." —*Bob Nordin*

Former employee Janet (Jenson) Remington says, "I remember at Christmastime going up to the lounge in the corner on the second floor and just sitting and looking out the window down to Main Street on a Friday night. There was Christmas music out on the street. Bell ringers. Santa walking around. I loved sitting there and watching and listening to it all."

Civic Pride and Generosity

Throughout all their years in Marinette (including into the current century—witness Frank Lauerman III depriving the wrecking ball from having its way with the landmark Milwaukee Road depot), the Lauerman family contributed to the betterment of the city and its residents. The number of small generosities they bestowed discreetly and without fanfare is beyond measure. Take the well-known story of Joseph Lauerman coming upon a young boy behind the Stephenson Public Library fishing with nothing but a tree branch, a line, and a safety pin. Mr. Lauerman invited the angler over to Lauermans' sporting goods department, where he outfitted him with rod, reel, and tackle box. Scores of people experienced members of the Lauerman family quietly taking care of problems during times of need. A family is in a pinch due to illness? Extend their credit. A former employee lost his home to a fire? We'll take care of him. So-and-so's brother is out of work? Find something for him to do.

"They were very good people, there's no question about it," says Glen Nordin, former state auditor, who handled the books at Lauermans. "Their business might have suffered because they were probably too nice."

Children in Marinette were accustomed to invitations from the Lauermans like this one from 1927. | *EagleHerald Publishing, Inc.*

Remembering Lauermans

Frank Lauerman's business ventures often hatched from efforts to better the community as a whole. A case in point was the Bijou Theater, which opened in 1905 on Main Street, across from the store. The Bijou was built for the vaudeville audience, and Frank made every effort to attract the best in entertainment. The *Marinette Eagle-Star* reported that "many of the best plays on the road" came to Marinette by way of the Bijou. But in 1914 Frank Lauerman and his business partner Daniel Madigan sold the Bijou to Nathan Ascher of Chicago, who promptly converted it into a movie theater to accommodate the public's interest in the new medium. With seven other theaters in Marinette/Menominee, the Bijou's small size (fewer than four hundred seats) put it at a disadvantage. In 1924 the Bijou Theater was converted into retail space and offices. It is the only one of the eight competing theaters still standing today.

An ad for the Bijou from October 11, 1906. Who in the workaday world of humdrum Marinette could resist coming out to see the advertised jugglers and singers, the cartoonist, and, especially, Prof. Ike Singer's troupe of educated monkeys? | *EagleHerald Publishing, Inc.*

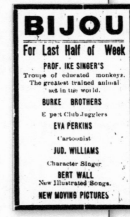

BIJOU

For Last Half of Week

PROF. IKE SINGER'S
Troupe of educated monkeys.
The greatest trained animal
act in the world.

BURKE BROTHERS
Expert Club Jugglers

EVA PERKINS
Cartoonist

JUD. WILLIAMS
Character Singer

BERT WALL
New Illustrated Songs.

NEW MOVING PICTURES

The Bijou Theater on Main Street at right, circa 1915. Note the painted sign on the wall of Lauermans across the street. Adjacent buildings would soon be razed to make way for the store's final expansion. | *Bob and Eva Kiefer*

Former employee Cindy Gressell remembers Ray Lauerman giving money and coffee to needy people at the lunch counter, while Dorothy Pronold, niece of longtime employee Laura Parent, singles out Frank Jr. and Henry Sr. as "extremely nice and down to earth. There was something about those people that you couldn't forget."

On a larger scale, though nearly as inconspicuous, Lauermans often showed great beneficence in its day-to-day business practices, as pointed out by the *Menominee Herald-Leader* in 1935: "During the World War, the Lauerman stocks were not marked up to fit a war market. This policy cost the firm a fortune in possible profits, but added an army of friends and customers."

Other company policies demonstrate a similar awareness of—and involvement in—the lives of community members. While today's stores push merchandise especially hard on major holidays, Lauermans closed its doors for even minor holidays, and for Catholic holy days as well. And holidays back then were celebrated on the days of the week they happened to fall—not just on weekend-extending Mondays. The store also closed for half-days for the funerals of important people in the community and for the annual M&M football game between Marinette and Menominee High Schools.

The Lauermans made more than their share of grand, public acts of charity as well, including a noteworthy series of donations by family sports-lovers. In 1921, Marinette and Menominee fielded a number of semiprofessional football teams, sponsored by area businesses. According to historian Larry Ebsch, Frank Lauerman and his son Ray signed Paul Christensen of Menominee to be the player/coach of the Twins, the team sponsored by the Lauermans. Christensen, a college teammate of Chicago Bears founder George Halas, guided the Twins in their rise to the 1921 league championship. At least one of their players made it to the pros:

Walter Niemann played center for the Green Bay Packers from 1922 to 1924.

In the fall of 1922, Frank Lauerman donated the land that became Lauerman Field to the city of Marinette. Lauermans store employees contributed one thousand dollars toward the building of facilities there. In December of the following year, under a headline reading "Christmas Gift for Marinette," the *Marinette Eagle-Star* reported that Frank Lauerman was to fund the construction of a 2,300-seat reinforced concrete grandstand on the north side of the field, as well as a concrete wall to surround the field, with two large gates for access to the stadium. The cost of the grandstand was $12,000, bringing the total cost of the stadium at that point to $25,000. When the city installed lights at the field in 1935, Marinette's high schools joined a select few Wisconsin campuses able to hold games after dark. Many people today have fond memories of taking a seat at Lauerman Field and cheering for the home team in the crisp autumn air of a Friday night. (The unusual concrete stands suffered damage from a fire beneath them and were razed in the mid-1970s.)

Over the years, athletic teams, schools, and churches continually benefited from the Lauermans' giving spirit. Young athletes often had the Lauermans to thank for their equipment and uniforms, the latter often direct from the Lauerman-owned Marinette Knitting Mills. In the mid-1950s, Frank Lauerman donated money for the installation of a new gymnasium floor at Marinette Catholic Central, insisting on the best materials money could buy. The floor is still in place today and in fine shape.

The field itself at Lauerman Field is also still in good condition. Both the public and the Catholic high schools used Lauerman Field for football games on Fridays and Saturdays, and over the years city celebrations and circus performances were held there as well. Residents recall Bob Crosby's big band performing at Lauerman Field in the 1960s.

After a new Marinette High School was built south of town in 1972, Marinette Catholic Central continued using the field for a couple of years, but without the grandstand, the mystique was gone. Catholic Central eventually moved its games to Higley Field at the new high school.

Kids kicking footballs around today at Lauerman Field may or may not know that the turf under their feet was at one time hallowed football ground, where players blocked and tackled and ran for thrilling touchdowns. The crowds cheered loud enough to be heard by every resident on Water Street and beyond. Many in that crowd had earlier in the day punched the clock at Lauermans store.

10

Advertising and Promotion

FROM THE VERY BEGINNING of their business ventures, the Lauerman brothers believed in advertising and always set aside a percentage of their profits for printer's ink. (And paint. Many an area farmer received free barn paint in exchange for including a Lauermans ad on the side of the barn facing the roadway.) Though their stated policy was to keep the advertising honest and without exaggeration, they did get a little carried away from time to time, as we shall see.

Though Lauermans occasionally advertised on the bottom edge of the local newspaper's front page (a once-common practice of retailers), Lauermans "owned" the back page of the *Daily Eagle* as early as the mid-1890s. Their use of the last page of the *Marinette Eagle-Star* continued throughout the store's existence. Customers routinely flipped to the paper's back page to see what "The Big Store with the Little Prices" had to offer.

Lauermans' advertising in the 1890s reflected the store's limited inventory at that time: envelopes, papeterie (stationery), dry goods, millinery, clothing, underwear, hosiery, ribbons/laces/embroideries, notions, baby carriages, umbrellas/parasols, glassware, crockery, and lamps. At that time four pounds of Gold Dust washing powder sold for twenty cents. Twelve

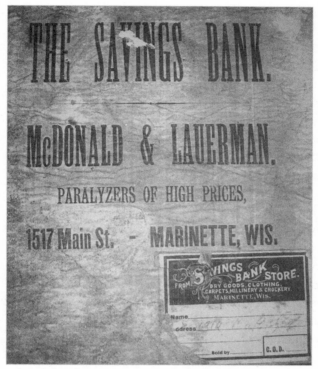

In the early days, the messages on posters and fliers were short and to the point. The message in this wall poster, from the brief McDonald & Lauerman incarnation of the store, could hardly be more succinct. | *Frank Lauerman III*

bars of German Family soap went for a quarter. Ink and pencil tablets were three cents, or two for a nickel. And how about the newfangled "glow night lamp": "No smell; no smoke; burns its own gas. One pint of oil lasts 200 hrs. 22c each."

During the 1899 Christmas season, Lauermans' toy offerings were categorized as follows: games, blocks, trumpets and musical toys, penny toys, rubber toys, mechanical toys, steam toys, tin toys, iron toys, China dishes, wooden toys, dolls, black boards, and harmonicas. On the same page in the *Daily Eagle* were Lauermans ads for pocketbooks and purses, Christmas cards, books, Bibles and prayer books, tree ornaments, medallions, and silk goods.

The frequent use of the term "better ones" makes us think that the copywriters were either brutally honest or didn't want to bother making the cheaper items sound a little better:

"Toy telephone: 24c. Better ones: 75c."

"Furniture sets in paper box: 8-piece sets: 5c. Better ones: 9c, 19c, 28c, 43c."

And dairy industry lobbyists must have put an end to the manufacture of this wonderful item: "Cows with movable heads: 20c. Better leather-covered ones: 48c. Cows, leather-covered that give milk: 90c."

Lauermans often named the bought-out companies and the circumstances behind the purchases that allowed them to advertise themselves as "Always a Little Cheaper than the Cheapest." Take this notice from 1899: "During this sale, the D. G. Bothwell and Co. stock bought at about 50c on the dollar will be placed on sale together with special bargains from our various departments."

Another common device was to specify how many items were on hand. "One lot" of handkerchiefs, or "two shipments" of umbrellas gave a rough idea of how long the supply—and the sale—would last. An ad for ladies' shoes from 1917 specified: "About 150 pairs, mostly small sizes, worth double and more than the price asked: $1.85."

Lauermans' early advertising was often neighborly and conversational, a technique that reinforced the prevailing impression of Lauermans as not just a store, but the shopper's friend. From April 1905: "It's largely a matter of personal preference with a woman as to where she trades. But the preference in nearly all cases is based on facts which appeal to her pocket book."

Another example is in this generous offer from 1903: "Telephone your orders to us. We will wait on you by 'phone and will fill whatever want you may express and send the goods to you promptly. Inability to reach Lauerman Brothers personally with convenience need not prevent your sharing the bargains offered."

But watch out for the scolding tone of the authoritative voice sometimes employed in Lauermans' ads: "To neglect such an opportunity would be a mistake of great proportion." And it

Who among us wouldn't say yes to this question that Lauermans asked in 1915? | *EagleHerald Publishing, Inc.*

Like many large stores of the era, Lauermans boasted an on-site millinery department, promoted here in an ad from 1905. Workers labored making ladies' hats, while customers sat at tables lined with mirrors, trying on the various creations. As always, Lauermans offered a wide range of style, price, and quality. | *EagleHerald Publishing, Inc.*

wasn't beyond Lauermans to occasionally disparage the competition, as in this ad from December 1899: "There is an endless variety here to select from in every grade. More styles, more colors and prettier goods than you'll find in all the other stores put together in the twin cities."

In the early 1900s, a trust existed between the advertisers and the public. Lauermans made it a sacred practice to live up to the claims made in its ads. No one seemed to mind an occasional exaggeration, however. The store posted this ad for shoes in 1904: "It makes no difference how small, nor how narrow your foot, we have the size and width to fit your foot. Price? Ah! That's an important issue, but one which is no obstacle for us to meet. We guarantee to give you every day in the year the best shoes ever made at cut prices."

Another grand claim, from 1915, was for Rexall Mucu-Tone, which would not only "disinfect and cleanse the entire mucous membraneous tract . . . destroy and remove the parasites which injure the membraneous tissues . . . soothe the irritation and beat the soreness, stop the mucous discharge, build up strong, healthy tissue and relieve the blood system of diseased matter," but also "stimulate the muco-cells, aiding digestion and improving nutrition until the whole body vibrates with healthy activity [and] bring about a noticeable gain in weight, strength, good color and feeling of buoyancy." And don't forget, if your body doesn't vibrate and become buoyant, "simply come and tell us, and we will quickly return your money without question or quibble."

For Lauermans' silver anniversary in 1915, an ad made the following claim: "This is to be the biggest sale of the firm's history. The bargains secured now will be remembered for twenty-five years to come." (Did anyone follow up on that claim in 1940?)

Some of the wording used in the early 1900s seems terribly quaint in this day and age. Even the littlest fellow today

"Push The Button and Rest"

FOOT REST SLIDES
BACK OUT OF SIGHT

Royal Easy Chairs
THE PUSH BUTTON KIND

Enjoy Luxury and omfort of one of these
Low Priced Easy Chairs.

ROYAL EASY CHAIRS
"THE PUSH BUTTON KIND."

These Chairs are national advertised and
special demonstration and sale of same is
made during this week of our Furniture Department.

A Royal Easy Chair will contribute something extra to your comfort if you want
"Head to Heel" comfort.

The exclusive patented Royal Push Button on the right arm of the chair operates a
noiseless, concealed mechanism which ad-
justs the chair back to the position you
desire and holds it there until you release it.

The Royal Easy Chairs are finished either Golden or Fumed Oak and upholstered in
genuine or art leather. Come and learn of
the low price and let us demonstrate these
chairs to you.

Beautiful SHOES

Add Charm
to an Exqui-
site Toilet.

When's the last time you added "charm to an exquisite
toilet" by buying a pair of shoes, as offered in this ad
from 1905? | *EagleHerald Publishing, Inc.*

The "Head to Heel" comfort described
in this 1915 ad sounds good. But must
you demonstrate the chair for us?
Couldn't we sit and try it ourselves?
| *EagleHerald Publishing, Inc.*

would balk at an ad that read, "Get the Little Fellow's Eas-
ter Togs at the 'The Big Store' and Save." (Though what boy
wouldn't want what was advertised in 1903: "Boys' blouse drab
washable waists, with sailor collar, whistle attached—85c"?)

The ads for adult clothing raise eyebrows today as well.
Corsets had "six supporter attachments," though for a dollar
less you could settle for just four. Some corsets included a "yoke
trimmed with one row of embroidery insertion, made with
very fine nainsook trimmed with embroidery medallions edged
with fine lace and insertions." Hmm. No, thanks.

Shirtwaists and knickerbockers were heavily advertised
in the early days. Petticoats were a necessity, too. The ads
described them as "trimmed with a solid 11-inch flounce of

German valencienne lace," "with scalloped dust ruffle," or "trimmed with two rows of torchon lace insertion."

For the men there were "colored shirts, mostly soft bosom, some with two collars and extra pair of cuffs." An ad from February 20, 1926, promoted: "Men's Fleece Lined Drawers—Drawers have reinforced gussett, self facing, tie back, ribbed cuffs on ankles." They don't make 'em like that anymore.

Wooden snow shovels made sense—many of the sidewalks were made of wood, too, in 1915.
| *EagleHerald Publishing, Inc.*

In the *Marinette Eagle-Star* of March 20, 1915, Lauermans announced a weeklong sale on nationally advertised goods. Allying oneself with the big companies was a new practice. As the ad explained: "There was a day, not so long ago, when you knew little of what you bought, who made it, or where it came from. Oatmeal was just oatmeal; cooking utensils just pots and pans. Today you ask for Kellogg's Corn Flakes, Wear-ever Aluminum cooking utensils, Colgate's toilet preparations. You know who makes them, you know where the factory is, you know what goes into the goods and what they will do for you."

The national advertisers provided Lauermans with samples of their goods, instructive displays, booklets, and promotional items. Many of the products from that era are still on the market today: Campbell's soups, Kellogg's cereals, Old Dutch Cleanser, Jell-O. Other brands have fallen away: Asbestol Leather Gloves, Packer's Tar Soap, Pebeco Tooth Paste. Still others are gone because the products themselves are obsolete: Koh-I-Noor Dress Fasteners, Victor Victrolas, Perfection Oil Heaters.

With all this attention on nationally advertised products, it's important to note that Lauermans continued to deal in locally raised and crafted merchandise. The "Something for Everyone" motto remained.

Lauermans occasionally pleased the crowds by offering samples, souvenirs, or gifts. For the tenth anniversary, in 1900, the company offered: "Beautiful aluminum souvenir. One to each customer, given to all those calling at our store. None given to children, so do not send children after souvenirs on this day."

Lauerman's Valuable Stamps with Every Purchase

GENUINE **VICTOR** RECORDS
Phonograph

Regular **75c** Values

A Limited Number **10c** ea.

This Group Includes the Following Foreign Language Records.

| Polish, German, Bohemian, Finnish | Jewish, Swedish, Lithuanian |

Also a group of dance records, fox trots, waltz numbers, etc. **10c**

This 1928 ad promoted Lauermans' phonographs, along with records in a number of languages.
| *EagleHerald Publishing, Inc.*

Men's Newest Style Square Scarfs
The season's biggest hit are these high-grade scarf squares, made of beautiful lustrous silks in solid colors of navy, maroon, gray, tan and white with fancy figured and polka dot effects in harmonizing colors. Size about 36 in. square.
No. 27C20-2013—Each **$2.25**

Men's One-Fingered Leather Gloves
One-fingered mitten with warm brushed hair lining, full length, wrist with adjustable leather wrist strap. A popular style with hunters as well as the man who drives a car. Priced extremely low. Size 7¾ to 10¼.
No. 27F-2430—Priced at........ **$2.25**
No. 27F-2431—Mitt at same price.

While remodeling their home in rural Marinette County, Dawn and Mark Carviou found a Lauermans advertising supplement from 1926 stuffed behind a wall, many of the pages in pristine condition. For seventy years the pages had remained hidden. Men's scarves such as these have gone the way of the Model T, as have the one-fingered gloves seen here. | *Dawn Carviou*

Holiday parades provided advertising opportunities for businesses like Lauermans. This photo was taken at Pierce Avenue and Main Street in Marinette on July 4, 1913. Note the beautiful horses emblazoned with Lauermans signs. | *Bob and Eva Kiefer*

A grand and glorious ad for the twenty-fifth anniversary in 1915, complete with Greek goddesses in ornate surroundings, announced THE MOST STUPENDOUS SALE EVER ATTEMPTED. It ranked right up there with the best of Macy's or Marshall Field & Company. But why, oh why, did they start their long list of bargains with a fifty-cent "slop jar" selling for twenty-five cents? (And Macy's never would have included the item a few lines down: "Men's Coin Purse, slightly soiled.")

In April 1929 Lauermans announced its engagement of the facilities at WTMJ in Milwaukee for the purpose of sponsoring a nationally broadcast radio show. On Thursday nights at seven o'clock, listeners could tune in for a half hour of music featuring the "Indo-European instruments and music" of the Croatian Sextet, interspersed with commercials for Lauermans' stores and knitting mills.

The *Marinette Eagle-Star* reported on April 8, 1929, that "with the innovation this week in using radio advertising,

Lauerman stores are again leaders, being the only exclusive retail stores in the states they serve to use this method of reaching the people, and the fourth retail firm in the United States to adopt the radio as an adjunct to newspaper advertising." There is no record as to how long the Lauerman radio program remained on the air.

Contests were always sure to stir customer interest. As a teenager, Marinette resident Karen Waloway won a dinette set during the store's seventy-fifth anniversary sale after writing the winning entry to the "Why I like to shop at Lauermans" contest. Her timing couldn't have been better, for she was married shortly thereafter and needed the furniture.

The advertising staff was forever on the lookout for new ways to entice customers: double or triple stamps, decorative plates, wooden nickels, promotional stickers. The best incentive, however, was customer satisfaction, and the money-back guarantee was the best way to ensure a happy shopper. Sometimes, though, the promotion of said guarantees bordered on the ridiculous. In 1915, the store offered silver-plated "State Souvenir" spoons for ten cents apiece with the following guarantee: "If for any reason the spoons you buy do not give satisfactory service, bring them back and we will give you new ones for them." Unless you held it upside-down, how could a *spoon* disappoint?

Each promotional spoon was "guaranteed." | *EagleHerald Publishing, Inc.*

Premiums and free gifts weren't the only methods of drawing customers to the store. Lauermans frequently offered free performances, demonstrations, or lessons in order for the public to better understand how to use the products they were buying. At times, curious customers watched as craftsmen plied their wares on the scene. In 1924 blind rug weavers demonstrated their skills in the corner window, and onlookers were invited in from the sidewalk to purchase the finished products.

At other times Lauermans advertised cooking demonstrations by representatives from the West Bend Company, samples from the latest products from Kellogg's of Battle Creek, and instruction on how to keep your feet in good shape from Dr. Scholl's of Chicago. During the 1920s Lauermans offered home demonstrations of "radio receivers," floor models in ornate wooden cabinets. Hearing beautiful music in one's usually quiet home led to quick sales.

In one of the more unusual publicity campaigns, as a draw for the fiftieth anniversary in 1940, Lauermans put out a call for pennies minted in 1890, the year of the store's founding. Customers were given a premium for each penny brought in.

ALL NEXT WEEK

An Invitation
to meet
Miss Betty Van Gasse
of the Richard Hudnut Salon
Fifth Avenue New York
who brings you the latest news
in beauty fashions

The HUDNUT SALON

Visit Our Toiletries Section

Consult Miss Van Gasse, without obligation of course. Accept a double size value of the new Du Barry Rose Cream Mask . . . a "pick-up" treatment which not only clears and firms your skin, but also imparts a youthful radiance . . . special for $1 . . . only during Miss Van Gasse's visit.

Toiletries . . First Floor

From 1936, a cordial invitation to consult with an expert on beauty and elegance being flown in from New York. Who in Marinette could resist? Many of the finest stores continue this practice at cosmetics counters today. | EagleHerald Publishing, Inc.

The pennies were kept in a box that remained in the office for years. Betty Sladek remembers Lloyd Dufresne reaching in and giving her a handful.

Jeff Behrendt took the reins as advertising manager in 1971 and came up with some unique promotions for the store, including his famous "Balloon Drop." Coupons were placed inside inflated balloons, which were dropped at a designated time from the viaduct over Vine Street to the crowd below. Most of those who secured a balloon—and some arrived with long-handled fish nets to increase their odds—redeemed coupons for a cup of coffee or a 7-Up at the lunch counter; others walked away with hundred-dollar gift certificates. "It was the talk of the town," says Bruce Leannah. "There were tons of people." Two groups were far from thrilled with the event, however: the office workers who had to blow up all the balloons, and the overworked staff at the lunch counter who had to fulfill the coupon orders.

Under Behrendt, Lauermans offered "Invitation Only" sales on furniture, TVs, and appliances. On a night when the store was normally closed, select customers were allowed in with the presentation of the invite received by mail. "The people thought they were getting something special," says Jerry Blohm, "and I suppose they were."

The store looked for ways to make people feel they were a part of something unusual or exclusive. The crowds responded well to "Saturday Only" sales and "After Supper" specials. Lauermans had a knack for seeing dry periods on the calendar and making holidays out of them: "Summer Sidewalk Daze" and "Fall Festivals" drew in eager customers every time.

The sidewalk sale always did well in the summer. Hauling the merchandise out to the sidewalk was no small task; customers were guaranteed of finding good bargains because the more that was sold, the less work there would be in dragging the stuff back in later. "I remember being at the sidewalk sale one time," says Roberta Kairys, a cousin of mine, "and your father and my father were talking. Your dad said, 'If we put a price of 49 cents on a shirt, nobody buys them, but if we say they're two for a buck, they fly off the shelf.' I'll always remember him saying that."

Remembering Lauermans

"You'd find one-of-a-kind items as you rummaged at the sidewalk sale. I wish I knew then what I know now about vintage clothing." —*Linda Murphy*

Surely the few stores today that still conduct sidewalk sales don't follow Lauermans' method of making dressing rooms out of refrigerator boxes with doors cut into the sides of them. It wasn't easy trying on a pair of pants inside a far-from-sturdy cardboard box.

Lauermans never missed a beat when it came to advertising and promotion. Creative minds were always at work: A "Twenty-five Cent Sale" on the store's twenty-fifth anniversary. Useful items such as wooden rulers, plastic thermometers, and metal shoe horns engraved with Lauermans' name and logo given as gifts with receipts of purchase. When you have "Something for Everyone," cash registers chime from dawn until dusk.

With the right promotion, Lauermans could sell anything. It's a surprise that during one of the sidewalk sales they didn't find a way to sell the sidewalk.

As late as 1983, Lauermans issued wooden nickels, a throwback to the 1930s when merchants and banks commonly used such tokens for promotional purposes.
| *Charles J. Lauerman Family*

11

Other Business Interests

DURING THE 1920S a trend took hold across the country in which department stores branched out into businesses beyond their former boundaries. In fact, by 1929 more than 60 percent of all department stores in the United States were chain stores.

Lauermans had already acquired Marinette Knitting Mills in 1904 and had made it into a profitable enterprise, with additional plants coming later to Oconto and Appleton. In 1926 Lauermans chose the city of Oconto to be the home of its second retail store, with more to follow in other Wisconsin cities, as well as in Upper Michigan and in Iowa. Some of the owners' sons were now of age and could take active roles in the management of these satellite stores.

Marinette Knitting Mills

In 1904, the same year the Lauermans' Big Store opened on Dunlap Square, Frank J. Lauerman organized Marinette Knitting Mills. The operation began in a small building on Pierce Avenue before moving to a larger site on Wisconsin Street,

The Marinette Knitting Mills building at Pierce and Daggett, seen here in the early1900s, still stands today but is in disrepair. | *Bob and Eva Kiefer*

where by 1906 twenty-five people were employed. A fire in January 1909 forced the business to move into the M&M Light and Traction Company building at the Wisconsin end of the Interstate Bridge (site of the current Elks Club). Construction of the plant at Pierce Avenue and Daggett Street began immediately, and the business opened there on January 1, 1910.

The sweaters and knit dresses produced in Marinette by the "Aristocrats of Knitted Wear" were top-shelf items at the nation's finest clothing stores. With the opening of a second knitting mill in Oconto in 1913—in the old Turner Opera House at Adams Street and Superior Avenue—Marinette Knitting Mills became one of the area's largest employers, with an especially large workforce of women. Branch offices in New York, Chicago, and Los Angeles enabled the company to sell its products in every state of the Union and to reach world markets as well. Business peaked in 1920, with more than four hundred employees in the two plants.

On April 20, 1935, the *Menominee Herald-Leader* suggested, "If you are a wee bit homesick the next time you drop in at Manila or Honolulu or Shanghai or Tokyo, look in the windows of the biggest and best store for a reminder of home. There you will see a fine display of the famous garments for women made by the Marinette Knitting Mills."

That newspaper article continued by addressing the eternal question of where styles and fashions originate, claiming that the designs used at Marinette Knitting Mills didn't come from New York or Paris, but from a room at the Marinette factory. According to the article, "Helen Gustafson, the artist designer, has for years made a study of her special work, and the garments she makes are personally modeled by her, woven and refined until they are ready, in her estimation, to fill the demands of the women's market." Gustafson got final approval from company vice president and general manager L. C. Wemple before the designs were put into manufacture sixty to ninety days before the season openings.

Helen Gustafson didn't always do the modeling. Bringing an unusual flavor to the local classified ads of that era, this notice appeared in the *Marinette Eagle-Star* of April 8, 1914: "Wanted: Young lady with good figure as model to try on sweater coats in our factory. Must have 38 inch bust and be about 5 feet 8 or 9 inches tall and of neat appearance."

Imagine the pride of the Marinette workers when they saw their clothing on the models in advertisements for cosmetics or cigarettes in the leading magazines of the 1930s. Or upon reading this April 7, 1935, ad in the *New York Times* fashion pages for Russeks of Fifth Avenue, one of the country's most famous women's clothing emporiums: "Russeks, recognizing the importance of smartly styled quality knitted sports clothes for discerning women, chooses Marinette's EXCLUSIVELY."

In the 1940s, Marinette Knitting Mills had exclusive rights to produce the Disney clothing line. Joan Alfredson

Joseph Lauerman Jr. managed
Marinette Knitting Mills.
| *EagleHerald Publishing, Inc.*

remembers her father, Joseph Lauerman Jr., flying to Southern California to meet with Walt Disney himself.

In 1951 Marinette Knitting Mills became embroiled in a contentious strike. On July 12, 135 members of the International Ladies Garment Workers union—90 percent of the mills' workforce—took to the picket line. Among the items at issue were a pay increase, more vacation time, paid hospitalization insurance, and the promise of an all-union shop. Striking workers didn't restrict their activities to the mill on Pierce Avenue; pickets surrounded Lauermans store as well.

"I remember trying to get out of the store, and you couldn't get out—they'd slam the door back in your face," recalls Jerry Blohm. "I remember F. J. Lauerman walking the aisles saying, 'They can't do this to me.'"

The strike raged on, with news reports of vandalism, verbal assaults, and physical scuffles. After nearly four months, on Monday, October 29, a joint statement was issued by Joseph Lauerman Jr. and union vice president Morris Bialis. Terms of the settlement were not made public, although they were said to be satisfactory to both parties.

The 1958 book *Diary of a Strike* by Bernard Karsh details the events leading up to the strike, its course, and the aftermath. Many in the Lauerman family question the account of the strike as described in the book, claiming that the workers were not unhappy with their salaries and working conditions and were drawn into the strike by out-of-state union forces who wanted to bring down the business that continually outperformed unionized mills elsewhere.

This Milwaukee Boston Store display (date unknown) featured products made at Marinette Knitting Mills. | *Joseph A. Lauerman Jr. Family*

After the strike, the company struggled. To keep up with the competition, they installed new machinery. An ad campaign in *Life* magazine proved to be an expense not recouped in sales. In 1960, one year after the death of Frank Lauerman, Marinette Knitting Mills was sold to Harmon Juster, and it thereafter operated under the name Harmon Knitwear. In 1964 the mill gained national attention with the "topless swimsuit" designed there by Rudi Gernrich, at the time considered one of the top five fashion designers in the country. (Today Gernrich's creations fetch thousands of dollars on eBay.)

Business failed to flourish, however, and the mill on Pierce Avenue closed its doors in 1974. Today the building is owned by a local businessman. Plans by the city to develop the property fizzled in the fall of 2011. The building is currently for sale.

The Satellite Stores

By the early 1930s Lauermans had possession of fifteen satellite stores. The mother store's wholesale operation in Marinette led to associations with smaller stores near and far, and these associations occasionally resulted in business takeovers when the small stores fell on hard times. It was Lauermans' practice to buy a business, sell all existing stock, remodel the store, and restock it with merchandise of its choosing. Often the former workers, even the former managers, were offered a chance to return to their posts.

Though owned and operated by Lauermans, the satellite stores maintained a degree of independence not always advantageous to the organization as a whole. The Manistique store, for instance, sold Speed Queen appliances, while in Marinette the store handled strictly Maytag products. Had the businesses worked together better they could have purchased in larger lots and sold for less.

Some of the satellites—Sturgeon Bay, Two Rivers, St. Ignace, and Iron Mountain, for instance—had very brief runs, and little is known about them. In the early 1930s a Lauermans store in Newton, Iowa (Maytag's corporate headquarters), burned down before it had a chance for success. Many satellite stores had moderate to long runs, however, and were significant to their communities. As in Marinette, people in Shawano, Escanaba, and elsewhere responded to Lauermans' way of "buying for less and selling for less."

Oconto, Wisconsin

Lauermans' first satellite store opened in 1926 in the building formerly occupied by the Goodrich & Martineau Company at the southeast corner of Superior and Main in Oconto. The first floor of the old brick building offered groceries, men's clothes, fabrics, dishes, and gifts. On the second floor were

An artist's rendition of the Oconto Lauermans store | *EagleHerald Publishing, Inc.*

ladies' clothes, the business office, and the restrooms. James A. Ladd was the store's first manager. The Oconto store employed fifteen clerks, three of whom worked in the office handling cash exchanges made via pneumatic tubes shooting from the first floor to the second. Like the other Lauermans stores of the time, the Oconto store offered free and frequent delivery, with Pete Hazen making the rounds.

James Hermsen, a longtime Oconto schoolteacher, worked at the store in Oconto in the late 1930s, pulling a paycheck of fourteen dollars for toiling six days and one night a week. He worked in the first-floor men's department for manager Bud Casper, whose father was the Lauermans' district manager overseeing all the satellite stores. Hermsen remembers his father-in-law, manager Awalt Falk, frequently traveling to Marinette for daylong buying ventures and returning to Oconto with men's suits and other items purchased at the parent company's wholesale.

Other Oconto store managers over the years included Francis J. Martineau, Irving Bitzer, "Beaner" Picard, and Malcolm Cardiff. The Oconto store went out of business in 1973, and the building was demolished shortly thereafter. The Schultz Brothers dime store was erected on the adjacent property. Today that building houses the Oconto Pharmacy; its parking lot is the site of the former Lauermans store.

Waterloo, Iowa

On June 11, 1927, in what may have been his boldest business move since the founding of the original store in Marinette, F. J. Lauerman purchased the fixtures, stock, and accounts receivable of the Paul Davis Dry Goods company at Commercial and Fourth Streets in Waterloo. Built in 1924, the eight-story Davis Building (also known as the Hawkeye Building and the Caward Building) initially provided 105,000 square feet of floor space. Lauermans signed a long-term lease with the owner, the Massachusetts Mutual Life Insurance Company of Springfield, Massachusetts, securing the use of the first five floors and half

The store in Waterloo, Iowa, was the biggest of all the Lauermans stores.
| *EagleHerald Publishing, Inc.*

of the sixth, as well as the basement. (Lauermans eventually expanded to the seventh and eighth floors.)

Frank Lauerman must have felt a great need to stake a claim in Iowa. Fred Wray, representing the Davis Company, said, "The price paid for the store is the best offer I have received. It is somewhat larger than I had expected to be able to obtain." Not only was the Waterloo operation geographically distant from Marinette, but the building was bigger than the mother store, and, with a population of nearly fifty thousand, its surrounding community was much larger than Marinette. F. J. Lauerman's son Raymond took charge as manager of the business in Waterloo.

The store included a cafeteria that had served 170,000 meals in the previous year. The ornate fixtures within were said to have no equal in the entire Midwest. At the grand opening of the store on July 7, 1927, the ladies' dresses made at the Marinette Knitting Mills sold out completely, and customers had to be satisfied with promises of more to be delivered as soon as possible.

The Iowa store remained in business until June 1938. The *Waterloo Daily Courier* wrote on March 10 of that year that "no other firm is buying the Lauerman stock and fixtures, which will be disposed of in the regular course of business." The building sat empty for six years before the J. C. Penney Company moved in.

The building was razed in 1974. Today a convention center stands at the site.

Menominee, Michigan (The Lloyd Wonder Store)

Marshall B. Lloyd made his fortune through a series of inventions: a mechanical fishing spear, a combination scale and bag holder, a spring bed, and a home heating device. Most advantageous to his illustrious business career, however, were his inventions of various weaving machines, which led to his manufacturing companies producing woven wire materials and wicker furniture.

Twice elected mayor of Menominee (1913–1917), Lloyd was considered "the King of Menominee" by many city residents. So, when the Wilson-Henes Department Store burned on the night of February 24, 1924, the city looked to Lloyd for help in replacing the vital merchandiser on Sheridan Road (now First Street). He responded to the call with a plan to build the glorious Lloyd Wonder Store. Fifteen hundred members of the community bought stock at one hundred dollars a share. Lloyd himself invested $400,000 to build a "store to end all stores."

"Nothing but the best" was the order of the day, and Lloyd spared no expense. Everything from doorknobs to window casings were ornate. Grand and lavish entryways, cabinetry, and showcases were installed, along with eight thousand dollars' worth of mirrors. The three-story structure included a theater with the first "talkies" sound system north of Milwaukee.

The Lloyd Wonder Store in
Menominee, Michigan
| *EagleHerald Publishing, Inc.*

The grand opening was heavily promoted and greatly anticipated. The day after the store opened on October 12, 1926, the *Marinette Eagle-Star* described a "pent-up enthusiasm . . . bursting forth in glorious celebration" at "the greatest event in the history of Menominee." More than ten thousand people gathered to witness a spectacular parade with marching bands, speeches, and cheering. One orator stated that the building was "more than stone, steel, and concrete. It lives, breathes, pulsates. It is now and ever will be the heart of Menominee."

But within a year, Lloyd, whose health had been faltering, was dead at age sixty-nine. In July 1928, less than two years after the truly grand opening, Lauermans bought the Lloyd Wonder Store for the tidy sum of $600,000. More than seventy auditors descended on the building to inventory the existing merchandise. The managers at the Lauermans store in Marinette worked nights at the store in Menominee, readying it for business under the new management.

Due to the proximity of the mother store, the Lloyd Store was stocked with different lines of merchandise than what was offered in Marinette, the guiding principle being, "If you can't find what you want over here, then you're sure to find it over there." Henry Lauerman, son of Joseph Lauerman, was appointed manager of the Lloyd Store. Lauermans retained the

For a number of years, merchandise was advertised side by side for Lauermans and Lloyd's, as in this *Marinette Eagle-Star* ad from April 10, 1931. | *EagleHerald Publishing, Inc.*

services of Edgar A. Guensberg, Lloyd Store assistant manager, at that same post.

Under Lauermans, the Lloyd Store remained in business for more than ten years, but in 1939 came the news that the firm was "planning to vacate." Marinette and Menominee were just not big enough to sustain two department stores of such stature.

Montgomery Ward took possession of the building next, sharing the basement space with an A&P grocery store into the 1950s. In later years, Fish Net and Twine Industries used portions of the store for manufacturing purposes. The Lloyd Theater operated for years after the adjacent store went empty; its screen finally went dark in 1997.

The Lloyd Building, so beautiful in its prime, today suffers a slow and agonizing deterioration. The theater area, with the ticket office and many original features still intact, is now an antiques mall. A number of businesses have shown interest in the vacant store. Perhaps it's not too late for an industrious enterprise to restore some of the grandeur that was present for a brief time in the 1920s, back when the Lloyd Store was a genuine wonder.

Shawano, Wisconsin

The Lauermans opened a store in the former Hayter Company building at 214 South Main Street in Shawano in 1929. Under the lease agreement, the Shawano Telephone Company was allowed to continue occupation of its quarters in the building.

Remembering Lauermans

"I remember a tin basket on a stick being raised by a clerk to a cashier in the loft. They passed the basket back down again with receipts and change."
—*Sally McGee Zander*

The former Lauermans building on Main Street in Shawano today | *Geralyn Leannah*

The store was managed by Emil Otto, who held the post for many years. Managers at Lauerman satellites in Manistique, Michigan, and Clintonville, Wisconsin, trained under Otto in Shawano. From 1959 through 1974, Ray H. Schuster served as manager in Shawano. Tom Peterson was the last to take the helm there.

In 1973 the contents of the store were moved to smaller quarters across the street, into a former A&P grocery store. If the move was made to ensure long-term commercial success, it failed, for the Shawano concern was dissolved by the end of the decade.

A hardware store does business today in the building at 209 South Main. The original Lauermans building still stands across the street, empty and in disrepair.

Manistique, Michigan

In 1929, Lauermans bought the stock of Neville & Raredon, formerly the L. Rosenthal Store, in Manistique. For years manager Leonard Harbick was the driving force behind this Lauermans store. Harbick had started with the firm in Marinette in 1926 and learned the managerial ropes at the Shawano store. He took charge in Manistique in 1933. Another in a long line of Lauermans managers who seemed to spend more time at the store than at home, Harbick instilled great loyalty in his employees. "People loved working for him," his son Richard recalls.

At the age of eight, Richard Harbick made ten cents an hour doing odd jobs at the store for his father. He worked there through his high school and college years. Richard managed the toy department as an eighth-grader, and his sister Helen did the same some years later.

After a fire gutted the interior of the Manistique store in 1948, the parent company wanted to dissolve the business and find a place for Leonard Harbick again in Marinette. Harbick, however, resisted the idea, insisting on rebuilding the Manistique store. A man of many talents, Harbick himself built the counters and much of the furniture. "I know he did," says Richard Harbick, "because I had to varnish it."

The Manistique Lauermans, originally Winkleman's Department Store, competed with J. C. Penney's and the nearby People's Store. Lauermans is remembered for offering better selection and better service than the others. It remained in business into the late 1970s. The building, at 244 Cedar Street, is shared today by a bank and a home nursing association.

Waupun, Wisconsin

In 1929 Lauermans started business in the former Rank Store at 400 East Main Street in Waupun. The store later expanded to include the space at 402 East Main. Eugene Fitzgerald was the manager. An ad in the local newspaper called Lauermans "The Complete Family Store," listing ready-to-wear, dry goods, footwear, linoleum, men's and boys' clothing, groceries, and fresh meats. "Bring your eggs to Lauermans," urges an early ad. Simply call 114 to get the "highest prices in trade."

Started with great promise, the Lauermans in Waupun didn't last ten years. The building still stands. Since 2007, the first floor has been the home of the Golden Cup Café.

Clintonville, Wisconsin

Carl Schroeder, manager for the entire thirty-two-year run of the Clintonville store, started in Shawano under Emil Otto. A sizable operation initially, Clintonville's Lauermans scaled back the grocery and other departments in its later years.

Since the store's closing in the 1960s, the Lauermans building at 47 South Main Street has housed a youth center, an electronic game emporium, and, most recently, The Juice Bar, which offered health products and wellness classes. In 2008 owner Jenny Peterson lamented the remodeling done by prior occupants. The hardwood floors, the many windows, and the elevated office quarters were gone. So was the stairway just inside the main entrance that once led to the basement.

> *Remembering Lauermans*
>
> "Lauermans was very important to Clintonville, as its price range was better for some people." —*Patricia Schroeder-Burton*

"My classes are in the basement," said Peterson. "How I'd love to have those stairs right there in front."

The building is now empty and for sale.

Escanaba, Michigan

The Ed Erickson Company, at the time one of Escanaba's oldest retail establishments, was sold to Lauermans in March

A view of downtown Escanaba, around 1930. Lauermans is on the left. | *Rob Romero*

1928. The Lauermans store in Escanaba began under the management of James A. Ladd. In 1937, Ladd gave way to Hal Gerletti, who manned the post for more than twenty years. Chuck Boyle, grandson of Charles Lauerman, assisted Gerletti in Escanaba before moving to Marinette to take charge of the men's clothing department there. In 1959, Gerletti himself moved to the Marinette store as manager of the notions, domestics, yard goods, and candy departments. The store in Escanaba closed in the early 1960s.

More than any of the other former Lauermans stores outside Marinette, the brick building at 720 Ludington Street in Escanaba has retained its original charm. In 1998, the Eighth Street Coffee House opened in the former Lauermans building. On the day after Thanksgiving in 2008, owner Rob Romero allowed me to explore the building.

On entering, I immediately came upon a small shop filled with antiques and curios, housed in Lauermans' old refrigerated "Fur Room." Through another door, the brightly lit café offered an interesting menu, artwork on the walls, kid-friendly activities, and a concert stage for musical guests.

Romero led me to the basement, where many pieces of Lauermans memorabilia remained: the boiler room, the freight elevator, jewelry cabinets. Scrawled names of early employees were still visible on support beams overhead: Bill Sauers, Frank Sauers, Larry Boucher. Romero pointed out a beautiful advertising poster from the 1930s, recently uncovered from its hiding place behind a boarded-up display window.

Since Lauermans' closing in the 1960s, the Escanaba building has gone through many changes. The first floor was a "hippie-hangout" coffeehouse in the 1970s and later a cabinetry shop. A chapter of the Vietnam Veterans of America has occupied rooms there, and the place has been the headquarters for a variety of political groups. For a number of years, the

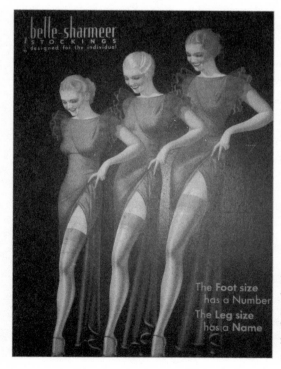

This advertising poster was found beneath a sheet of plywood covering a display window in the Lauermans store in Escanaba.
| *Rob Romero*

basement has been the headquarters for the Upper Peninsula Model Railroad Club; the elaborate layout they've constructed down there is a sight to behold.

I was sad to hear in 2012 that the Eighth Street Coffee House was no longer in business. Considering the building's unique qualities and long history, however, I expect a going concern will come to occupy the space that once was Lauermans. Rob Romero told me that a ghost is rumored to haunt the premises. If so, it roams a place with old touches remaining from the Lauermans era: a crank-out awning over the sidewalk out front, spacious display windows, a grand hardwood staircase to the basement. Lauermans had a good home in Escanaba.

The Burns Stores

This account wouldn't be complete without a note about the Burns Stores of Upper Michigan. From the 1930s into the 1950s, Frank Lauerman Jr. invested in Al Burns's department stores in Newberry, Sault Ste. Marie, and other cities. Burns bought his merchandise from Lauermans' wholesale. Frank Jr. became Burns's partner. The Burns Stores were successful enterprises into the 1960s.

By buying merchandise in great quantities, Lauermans was able to lower its costs and sell for less. The large number of satellite stores allowed Lauermans to buy in tremendous lots, putting the company at a distinct advantage over the competition.

Many of the smaller stores, however, didn't survive beyond the post-Depression years. By 1966 stores remained only in Marinette, Shawano, Manistique, and Oconto. By the late 1970s, Marinette stood alone.

Spokesmen for Lauermans continually stressed the point that their satellite stores were not part of a chain-store complex. Each individual store did its banking with local institutions, took full part in local civic activities, and assumed its share of the responsibilities and costs of public enterprises. It's no wonder that Lauermans' satellite stores are still remembered fondly in cities scattered across Wisconsin, Iowa, and Upper Michigan.

12

The Store's Demise

THE TIMES—and people's shopping habits—changed. In the twentieth century's last two decades, one large department store after another closed its books and its doors and went out of business. Hudson's, Marshall Field & Co, Wanamaker's, Gimbels, Bloomingdale's. Some were absorbed by the May Department Store Company or Macy's; others were simply dissolved. In 1987, Lauermans, too, bowed to the pressure applied by the chain stores and shopping malls.

"People's values were changing," explains Jeff Behrendt, advertising manager during the 1970s. "Every time a hearse went by, we used to say, 'There goes one of our good customers.' Lauermans was just a store whose time had come."

Fortunes started to change for Lauermans when the Tempo store came to Marinette's "twin city," Menominee, Michigan, in the late 1960s. The Pine Tree Mall followed in Marinette, putting a dent in business at the Menominee mall as well as Lauermans. "We complained when Kmart came to town," says Chuck Boyle, grandson of Charles Lauerman and manager of the men's department. "And we complained when Wal-Mart came to town. But people complained when Lauermans came to town, too."

The Pine Tree Mall and Tempo accelerated Lauermans' decline, but there were larger forces in play. Across the country the landscape had changed. All downtowns were suffering. Had the Lauermans pulled all the right strings, they might have extended their run a few years, but the company's fate had been decided. Chuck Boyle points out that "the Hudson Store in Detroit went under before we did, and in the 1950s it did more volume than any store in the world." Even midsize retail companies with more resources than Lauermans—firms counting fifty stores—were considered too small to make it against the giants, and one by one they folded.

Early in the company's history, the brothers made the decision to stay local, and for years Lauermans was content with being the "largest small-city store in America," family-run, and loyal to the people in its small corner of the world. "When everybody expanded and chain stores started, our predecessors didn't feel it was the route to go," says Henry Lauerman Jr. Though expansion to Iowa, Michigan, and other parts of Wisconsin did occur, a variety of factors thwarted long-term, consistent success. Using 20/20 hindsight, it's easy to see where Lauermans overreached here and weren't aggressive enough there. Just when they started making moves to expand their interests, the Great Depression loomed up and wreaked havoc on the plans. The similarities are many between Sam Walton's rise in Arkansas and that of the Lauermans in Wisconsin. With a few small changes in strategy—and a little luck—perhaps the Lauermans and the Waltons would switch places in business history, and today we'd see people flocking not to Wal-Marts, but to Lauer-Marts.

The palatial building on Dunlap Square, once the envy of any comparable enterprise, was another factor working against Lauermans' success. The two elevators, which cost a prohibitively high $18,000 a year to service, could not accommodate shopping carts, a problem Lauermans' competitors in single-story buildings did not need to deal with. With twelve-foot ceilings and poor insulation, the building's heating costs became enormous. Lauermans' annual electric bill ballooned to $70,000 by 1980. "The store is built like a rock," says Henry Lauerman Jr., "but it would have cost a bundle to make it efficient."

The end was difficult for everyone involved. The word *downsizing* wasn't a part of the lingo then, but that's what the company was doing. Even some very long-term employees had to be let go. "It wasn't easy releasing those people in the end," says Jeff Behrendt, "but they knew it was coming, and they understood." Departments were consolidated. TVs and dishwashers, for example, were moved together on the first floor. A St. Louis company took over the management of the shoe department. Whole areas of the store became empty space, off limits to customers.

In the 1970s, Lauermans was still doing a respectable business. By June 1983, the roster of employees was down to 112 people. By 1987, the number had dwindled to 28 full-time workers and a handful of part-timers.

The store's demise became official on May 19, 1987, when company president Henry Lauerman Jr. issued the following statement: "After over ninety-five years in the retail business in Marinette, our board of directors, acting upon direction given by our shareholders, made the decision to liquidate and close our downtown operation effective immediately." (Most of the ninety shareholders, all descendants of Joseph, Frank, and Charles Lauerman, lived outside the Marinette/Menominee area at the time.)

The men's wear department would continue in the Pine Tree Mall. The appliance and paint departments were to be sold and would not be part of the liquidation. Area businesspeople, including some Lauermans employees, formed a corporation to oversee the operation of a new home furnishings business. All else was to be liquidated within three months. Following Henry Lauerman's somber announcement, Chuck Boyle spoke of the building likely being razed.

On the last day of business at the store, longtime customers stopped in for one last chance to look around. A newspaper account of the final day included quotes from various principals. Frank Lauerman III said, "It's almost not describable. It's sad. It hurts." Charles Lauerman's daughter, Alice Boyle, said, "It's a real heartache to me. I can't believe it. I don't want to believe it."

Remembering Lauermans

"Sad. End of an era. I still hear comments: 'We're sorry you closed.'"
—*Jim Lauerman*

"It was horrible," Chuck Boyle remembers. "It was sadder for people like my mother and Aunt Monnie [Frank Lauerman III's mother]. You know, the last seven, eight years were very difficult, but we paid all of our bills. We didn't get into bankruptcy or anything. It was tough at the end, but there was nothing we could do."

"When they [the management] turned our pension plan into profit-sharing, that's when we knew something was wrong," says former employee Jerry Blohm. "They couldn't put any money into the plan because they weren't making money. There was no profit to share. At the meetings, guys were asking questions. They never gave any answers. What kind of answers could they give?"

"Perhaps our store closed fifteen to eighteen years too late," says Frank Lauerman III. Yes, and Willie Mays should have retired years before he finally did. But when you have a good thing going, who wants to pull the plug?

Employees remained on the scene after the store closed on September 5, 1987. | *Jerry Haines*

On Lauermans' last day, the Saturday of Labor Day weekend, September 5, 1987, Ray Pinkowski announced over the public-address system at ten minutes to five: "The store will be closing in ten minutes." This wasn't unusual. It was an announcement made every day at that time. Pinkowski returned five minutes later to announce: "The store will be closing in five minutes." At five o'clock sharp, once again Pinkowski's voice echoed through the building: "The store is now closed forever." I can imagine Joe, Frank, and Charlie looking down at the scene solemnly.

On Saturday, October 10, everything remaining in the store was auctioned off: merchandise, shelving, light fixtures, cash registers, everything.

"It was all done in such a hurry, and they could have made more money on that auction," Jerry Blohm recalls. "Some of the old-fashioned desks, hundred-year-old items, they were worth a lot. The cash registers were like beautiful pieces of art. Henry had a silver one in his office—one of the first ones the store ever had."

"I was disappointed with the way the auction went," says Jim Lauerman. "[The auction company] gave stuff away."

Lauermans auction notice, October 1987 | *Chuck Finnessy*

Lauermans retained Jeff Behrendt and Ralph Keller for six months after the store's closing to tie up leftover credits and debits. It was no easy task extracting payment from debtors who knew of the store's lame-duck status. Ultimately, many never paid what was due.

In spite of some of the ugly twists that occurred at the end, some people today are quick to take heart. "At one time, Prange's wanted to buy us," says Chuck Boyle's son Tom, "but we outlasted them."

"Just look at Prange's," adds Chuck Finnessy. "They were bigger, but they're all gone now, and Lauermans carries on. Henry Lauerman's furniture store is still going; Warren Heider's paint store had its start at Lauermans. CJ's Outlet just went out of business after many years. Abco Appliances was Jerry Blohm's."

Most of the employees did not receive much in the way of severance pay or pensions. Like most stores forced into closing, Lauermans went out with a fizzle. To their credit, Henry, Frank, and Chuck took many former employees with them into their new business ventures.

Thankfully, predictions of the store being torn down did not come to pass. Today, the Simply Charming boutique occupies much of the store's ground floor. Browsing patrons will recognize the beautiful marble tile floor, installed in 1935, and much of the original walls, windows, and ceiling—and the lovely mosaic tiles spelling out LAUERMAN BROTHERS at the entrances on Dunlap Square and Main Street.

"A hundred years later," says Frank Lauerman III, "the building is still as beautiful as it ever was."

The interior of the store today. Former Lauermans customers entering the boutique currently housed in the building at Dunlap Square can't help but notice the architectural components remaining from the days of yore: the pillars, ceiling, woodwork, windows, and marble floor are forever familiar as being "Lauermans." | *Michael Leannah*

The store's major entryways at Main Street and Dunlap Avenue feature mosaic floor tiles such as the one seen here. It's anyone's guess how many feet have trod upon these tiles since the opening of the store in 1904. | *Michael Leannah*

With so many cities' palatial department stores having been lost to wrecking ball and bulldozer, the citizens of Marinette can take pride in the splendorous building at the heart of their downtown. When the store closed in 1987, some saw its demolition as inevitable, but more than a quarter-century has passed without such incident, and the building's grandeur seems only to grow. Today both the store and adjacent wholesale building are vital interests, with retail establishments on the ground floors, resident apartments above, and parking at the basement levels. | *Michael Leannah*

Today, sadly, when a young person asks for directions in Marinette and is told to go to Lauermans and turn left, she'll likely say, "What's Lauermans?" How do you tell someone who wasn't there what Lauermans meant to Marinette? The store was once the hub of the entire city. No one could have guessed that a day was going to come—so soon!—when department stores would fall out of favor, and a place such as Lauermans would be as quaint and rare as one of the horse-drawn delivery wagons that used to serve the store.

The Lauerman Family Tree

Joseph Lauerman (1842–1911) married
Antoinette Kratochvil (1845–1886)
  Joseph Albert (1866)
  Frank (1869)
  Henry (1870)—died in infancy
  Anna (1871)
  Charles (1874)
  Marie (1876)—died in infancy

After the death of Antoinette, Joseph married **Annie Fucik**
  John (1894)
  Edward (1895)

Joseph Albert married **Amelia Besio** in 1892.
Two children died in infancy, Amelia in childbirth.
Joseph married **Cecilia Kellerman** in 1901.

  Henry (1902)—married Ruth Lamb
    Henry Jr. married Jackie Johnson
    Betsy married Richard Klatt
    Dorothy married Stokes Carden

  Catherine (1903)—married Gene Brennan
    Eugene Jr. married Patricia Thiel, later Lois Hays
    Thomas married Becky Maxwell
    Joseph married Sherry Keaton
    Mary Catherine married Mike Gallagher
    Michael married Jacklyn Conner

  Antoinette (1905)—married Alex Kasper
    Alex married LaNette Garcia
    Marie
    Cecelia married Don Lemersal
    Roger married Kathleen Schevers, later Mary Tietz

Joseph Jr. (1909)—married Geraldine Tulley
    Joan married Richard Alfredson
    Joe married Joan Wendel
    John married Janet Gibson
    Geraldine married Michael Seaman
    Tom married Mary Brodahl

Elizabeth (1910)—married Clarke Glavin
    Kathryn married Joe Gagliardi
    Jane
    Carol married William Warren

Ursula (1911)—married Edward Meyer
    Edward married Joan Gardipee
    Suzanne married Alan Hubbard
    John married Mary Bauer
    Ursula married William Thomasma
    Mary married Ronald Smits, later Don Coover III
    Catherine married Tom Tracy
    Theresa married Dante Kobek

Frank married **Nellie Faun** in 1893.

Joyce (1895)

Marshall Raymond (1896)—married Neva Lange
    Raymond, Jr. ("Nibbs") married Jane Reuter
    James married Maureen Pfankuch

Faith (1896)—married Robert Cleary

Frank Jr. (1898)—married Monica Barry
    Frank III married Lois Erdman
    Helen married John Musser

Lucille (1899)—married Frank McGinn
    Frank married Betty Rosenberry
    John married Frances Gaubinger

Nellie Faun died in childbirth in 1903.
Frank married **Margaret Quilty** in 1915.

Anna married **Henry Pfiester.**

Emily

Laura married John Scherer
  John
  Patricia married James Van Camp
  Mary
  Barbara

Mary married James Montgomery

Charles married Mae Marineau
  Ann married Donald Bretl
  Carol married Louis Stray
  Charles
  Robert

Frank married Leona Boivin
  Patricia married Terry DeGuzman
  Connie married Dane Warras

Charles married **Emma LeBlanc** in 1901.

Alice (1902)—married Francis Boyle
  Charles married Betsy Zylkowski (deceased 2004),
    then Connie Huss
  Francis married Charlotte Frankow
  Mary Faith married Val Johnson

Helen (1906)—married Thomas Moriarty
  Beth married John Richards

Charles F. (1913)—died in 1917

The Lauerman Brothers' Code of Ethics

There is no substitute for honesty.

Do not buy what you cannot pay for.

Discount every bill when due.

"Sell and repent," which simply means give
the buying public low prices. Sell at a small profit.
Then buy again with cash to replenish stock.

Advertise accurately and often.

Keep pace with the markets, the styles, and the trends of the times.

Buy for less to enable the store to sell for less.

Lamps, stoves, and dishes galore in the basement hardware department, circa 1910
| *Charles J. Lauerman Family*

The Names

For most of the store's run, the number of people on the payroll fluctuated in the 250–350 range, peaking at 440 in the 1940s. People came and left, some staying for a single summer, others for fifty or sixty years.

The following people worked at Lauermans for more than thirty years:

Joan Armstrong, Evelyn Barrett, Emma Bartels, Elsie Mae Bauer, Barb Baumgarten, Millie Belaire, Eva Bellemore, Jerry Blohm, Walter DeVoe, Elizabeth DeWane, Les Duescher, Lloyd Dufresne, Betty Dugan, Jean Eggener, Fannie Fillinger, Ella Fournier, Joyce Harteau, Rose Herning, Val Hruska, Harold Hoare, Cecil Hogan, Loretta Hornick, Lillian Kamin, Alfred Kaye, Eddie Krasnicky, Joe Kiefer, Sophie Kuntz, Gertrude LaFountain, Axel Larson, Flossie Larson, Anna Larson, Francis Leannah, Jesse Legault, Bertha Lemieux, Mary Mathy, Martha Mogensen, Art Nelson, Charles Neumeier, Laura Parent, Ray Pinkowski, Helen Poquette, Mavis Poquette, Lorraine Renton, James J. Schleihs, Myrtle Schroeder, Jen Shaver, Helen Shefky, Betty Sladek, Lenroy Sulk, Florence Theis, Les Topel, Lucille Trottier, and Millie Vieth.

Many an employee found a spouse through working at the store. There were a number of husband-and-wife teams with long histories at Lauermans, including:

Clem and Eva Bellemore, Art and Jane Bigger, Blanche and Charles Bilodeau, Ann and Jack Burke, Bernice and Cliff Brevitz, Cliff and Mary Chaltry, Bonnie and Jerry Haines, Irene and Warren Heider, Ed and Madeline Kieff, Erv and Joan Krukowski, Gertrude and Les LaFountain, Leona and Walter Pfiester, Barb and Harold Pierce, Helen and Wally Rademacher, Bill and Vi Ramsay, Signa and Ted Soderberg, and Les and Ellen Topel.

The following list includes Lauermans personnel who served at the store for at least two or three years. (Managers' names are in bold.) The personnel records are gone, so to list the names of all who ever worked for Lauermans would be impossible. (Some people suggest scanning an old telephone book, since nearly everyone in Marinette and Menominee worked at Lauermans at one time or another.) The names of employees from the early decades are especially hard to come by after all these years.

Every effort was made to make this list as complete as possible, with correct spellings and accurate job descriptions. Many employees jumped from department to department, or worked for two or more departments simultaneously. (Did Ray Pinkowski's mother have twins or triplets? Some days it seemed he was behind every counter.) I apologize for any inaccuracies that remain.

My only regret in making this list is my inability to convey the many glowing comments made about these people as their names surfaced in interviews. Some names—Eva Bellemore, Jean Vedra, Ed Kieff, Helen Blahnik, and Ella Fournier among them—made people time and again stop and say, "What a dear soul . . ."

Wayne Adams: domestics
Dan Althaus: furniture
Sophie Anilionis: linens
Marie Anderle: stationery, office/ school supplies, crockery
Mabel Anderson: ladies' ready-to-wear
Joan Armstrong: lingerie, linens, furniture
John Arendt: delivery
Evelyn Barrett: children's clothing
Tobin Barrette: maintenance
Monica Barry (Mrs. Frank Lauerman Jr.): jewelry and silverware

Emma Bartels: mail order
Helena Bates: lunch counter
Claudia Bauer: lunch counter
Elsie Mae Bauer: groceries, fabrics, notions, gift wrap
Joe Bauer: freight elevator
Barb Baumgarten: foundations
Rollie Baumgarten: drapery installer
Floria Baumler: fabrics, notions
Donald Beardsley: clerk
Robert Beauparlant: butcher
Harold Beecher: shoes
Augusta "Gusty" Behnke: lunch counter

Helen Behnke: religious items and gifts

Jeff Behrendt: advertising, credit

Norm Behrendt: elevator operator, warehouse

Millie Belaire: men's furnishings, accessories, Boy Scout supplies

Mike Beland: sporting goods and hardware

Clem Bellemore: furniture, warehouse

Eva Bellemore: stenographer

Joe Benesh: crockery

Norma Bergen: domestics

Leona Bergren: school/office supplies

Wally Bergstadt: shipping

Betty Beyer: stationery

Carol Beyer: lingerie

Dorothy Beyer: groceries, school supplies

Fred Bieber: maintenance

Lucille (Kapaun) Bieber: domestics

Art Bigger: TV/radio repair

Jane Bigger: linens

Alice Bilodeau: ladies' ready-to-wear

Bill Bilodeau: office boy

Blanche Bilodeau: switchboard operator

Charles Bilodeau: payroll

Helen Blahnik: stationery

Edwin Block: salesman

Otis Blohart: delivery

Jerry Blohm: electrical and appliances, "Maytag Man"

Jim Blohm: electrical and appliances

Pat Blohm: toys, jewelry

George Blondin: elevator operator

John Boatman: clerk

Dick Boivin: electrical and appliances

Art Bolshius: fire stoker

Barb Boneham: office

Scott Boren: electrical and appliances

Marion Borgwardt: paint and wallpaper

Jerry Borowski: warehouse, stationery, cameras, crockery

Herman Bostedt: butcher

Mildred Bothwell: housewares

Dorothy Boucher: paint and wallpaper

Chuck Boyle: men's furnishings

Jane Boyle: men's furnishings, candy, lunch counter, etc.

John Boyle: men's furnishings

Tom Boyle: men's furnishings

Tim Bradley: men's furnishings

Louella Braiway: clerk

Ann Bresnahan: linens

Elizabeth Bretl: drugs

Bernice Brevitz: crockery

Cliff Brevitz: maintenance

Joyce Bromund: lingerie

Alton "Brownie" Brown: electrical and appliances, "Maytag Man"

Jo Brown: warehouse secretary

Amelia Brusewitz: gift wrap

Clem Bruso: furniture warehouse

Mildred Buechler: lunch counter

Edith Bundy: paint and wallpaper cashier

Scott Bundy: electrical and appliances

Alfred "Al" Burby: interior décor, TVs, men's wear

Ann Burke: office

Jack Burke: advertising

Alice Bush: stationery, office/school supplies

Rachel Bushmaker: cameras, cards

Peggy Cahill: elevator operator

Ruth Cahill: toys

Ruthie Cairns: drugs, lunch counter

Kathy Callies: lunch counter

Louise Campbell: electrical and appliances

Gail Cardin: stationery, office/school supplies

Clara Carrigan: elevator operator, cashier/green stamps

Bob Carroll: assistant office manager

Mr. Casper: district manager of satellite stores in Wisconsin, Iowa, and Michigan

Frank Cervenka: shoemaker/shoe repair

Cliff Chaltry: sporting goods and hardware

Mary Chaltry: shoes

James Champley Jr.: men's ready-to-wear

Harold Charette: men's shirts, ties, hosiery, haberdashery

Homer Charette: floor coverings

Dorothy Charles: handkerchiefs, scarves, gloves

Hazel Chepeck: domestics, linens

Leo Chepeck: carpeting

Virginia Chmela: paint and wallpaper

Mr. Christenson: sewing machine repair

Alice Clark: stockings

Florence Cleary: billing

Robert E. Cleary: groceries

Lillian Coble: notions

Barb Collard: office

Millie Collard: electrical and appliances

Estelle Colvin: fabrics, notions

Lucille Combes: ladies' ready-to-wear, linens

Jake Cook: Blue Room/third-floor lunch room cook

Eva Cornell: shoes

John Corry: groceries

John Corwin: maintenance

Dione Coughlin: music

Dan Crocker: paint and wallpaper

Arlene Cummings: music

Nina Cummings: credit

Marge Davis: ladies' ready-to-wear

Jerry DeGaynor: music

A.J. DeLeers: credit office; handled legal work, wholesale business, and satellite stores

Blanche Dennis: office

Helen Dettmann: crockery

Walter DeVoe: men's furnishings, "The Hanes Man"

Elizabeth DeWane: religious items and gifts

Allison "Bud" Diebels: grocery

Lee Diercks: warehouse, stationery, cameras, crockery

Barb Dionne: foundations

Lillian Doman: billing

Al Doran: warehouse receiving clerk/ traffic manager

Connie Doran: office

Debbie Doran: switchboard operator

Ed Doran: sporting goods and hardware

Helen Doran: office

Mike Doran: floor coverings

Myrtle Doran: office, housewares

Alice Drees: crockery

Jo Drown: stenographer

Grace Drum: clerk

Lester Duescher: shoes, wholesale, men's wear/warehouse

Lois Duescher: stenographer, domestics

Jerry Dufresne: office boy

Lloyd Dufresne: office manager

Terry Dufresne: housewares

Betty Dugan: stationery, crockery

Estelle DuHaime: office

Loretta DuHaime: office

Amanda Dungan: furniture

Betty Dupuis: crockery

Francis Duquaine: paint and wallpaper

Bonnie Dura: elevator operator

Jean Eggener: cashier

Jerry Eggener: electrical and appliances

Gary Eick: maintenance

Laura Eisenman: cook
Tim Eland: furniture, warehouse
Marie Ellingson: clerk
Alvin Ellison: shoes
Carol (Peters) Emmes: office, filer
Wayne Emmes: music
Eugene Enderby: drapery installer
Betty England: office
Ethel England: crockery
Ann Erickson: shoes, jewelry and
    silverware
Mabel Eriman: office
Mabel Esterbrook: crockery
Nick Faber: stock clerk
Mary Falkenberg: advertising, switch-
    board operator, accounts payable
John Farnsworth: Santa Claus
Mike Faucett: office boy
Marty Feldson: elevator
Larrian Fifarek: shoes
Theresa Fifarek: music
Fannie Fillinger: printing, men's
    alterations
Laura Finn: seamstress
Chuck Finnessy: men's furnishings
John Fischer: salesman
Maude Fleming: ladies' ready-to-wear
Agnes Flink: crockery
Eunice Foley: shoes
Eddie Forslund: butcher
Ella Fournier: stationery, office/school
    supplies
Matthew Fournier: office clerk
Catherine Frink: handkerchiefs,
    scarves, gloves, jewelry
Suzy Frink: fabrics, notions
William Frink: salesclerk
Delmar Fritz: paint and wallpaper
Dewey Galleske: furniture, warehouse
John Garon: office boy, notions,
    children's clothing, lingerie, linens,
    warehouse

Tonnie Gauthier: lunch counter
Caroline Geniesse: office
Tom Gerbishak: floor coverings
Hal Gerletti: domestics, yard goods,
    notions, candy
Bob "Goose" Gibson: electrical/
    appliance
Louis E. Giese Jr.: linens, notions,
    warehouse
Dan Gignac: printing
Ethel Goddard: groceries, linens
Harold Goddard: driver/delivery
Ella Gordon: dress goods and silks
Bud Grace: drug department
    stockman
Lars Grace: hardware/housewares
Warren Grace: hardware, household
    utilities
Edith Gray: stationery, office/school
    supplies
Gertrude Greenwood: groceries
Katherine Grenier: office
Roger Grenier: shoes
Cindy Gressel: crockery, lunch
    counter, candy, etc.
Gene Groleau: Santa Claus
Yvonne Groleau: credit
Eleanor "Dolly" (Kopischke) Gruman:
    pharmacy, domestics, linens
Carol Grun: electrical and appliances
Herb Guimond: furniture, carpeting
Bror Gyllenberg: meats
Mary Gypp: linens
Wayne Haasch: warehouse, stationery,
    cameras, china and gifts
Mary Hagemann: credit
Art Haglund: paint and wallpaper,
    warehouse
Bonnie Haines: elevator operator,
    switchboard operator
Jerry Haines: warehouse, sporting
    goods and hardware

Marian Haines: toys, china, linens

Monica Haines: stenographer, hardware, advertising

Jackie Hansen: fabrics, notions

Loren Hanson: driver/delivery

Bob Harbick: Santa Claus

Michael D. Harpt: shoes

Norman Harpt: men's shoes, luggage

Joyce Harteau: lingerie

Ida Hartwig: charwoman

Cathy (Kiel) Hartzheim: music, candy

Jane Hass: lingerie

Dorothy Hatch: interior decorations/display

Alice Hearty: office clerk

Myrtle Heath: stock clerk, shoes

Bernice Heider: grocery

Irene Heider: furniture

Wally Heider: carpeting

Warren Heider: paint and wallpaper

Bonnee Lee Heim: lunch counter

Ed Henes: electrical and appliances, Lauermans' first "Maytag Man"

Rose Herning: linens, cashier/green stamps

Alice Hinz: cashier/green stamps

Bob Hinz: paint and wallpaper

Harold Hoare: electrical and appliances, office

Leatha Hoefgen: fabrics, notions

Betty Hoffman: paint and wallpaper

Monica Hoffman: music

Cecil Hogan: groceries, candy, gift wrap

Hannah Mae Holmes: shoes

Hazel Holtz: men's wear

Judy (Dugan) Hopfensperger: religious items and gifts

Frank Hornick: butcher

Loretta Hornick: religious items and gifts

Valuska "Val" Hruska: lunch counter

Franny Hubert: floor coverings

Roberta Huebner: candy, lunch counter

Millie Hultman: lunch counter

Joe Hutchinson: men's wear

Signa Huus: salesclerk

Jay Ihde: floor coverings

Lee Ihde: floor coverings

Agatha Jack: cashier

Maidie Jensen: groceries, bakery, candy, religious items and gifts

Martha Jenshok: crockery

Roger Jeranak: floor coverings

Violet Jessup: cashier

Patsy Johansson: clerk

Arthur Johnson: stock clerk

Carol Johnson: clerk

Clayton "Smokey" Johnson: electrician/maintenance

Ethel Johnson: draperies

Florence Johnson: domestics

George Johnson: maintenance, delivery

Grace Johnson: salesclerk

Kenny Johnson: delivery

Norm Johnson: maintenance, elevator operator

Oscar Johnson: shoes

Eleanor Josephson: seamstress

Byron Kaab: salesclerk

Eric Kaiser: printing

Lillian Kamin: accounts payable

Ray Kamin: maintenance

Katherine Kamps: billing

Mary Kamps: men's wear

Verne Kanter: billing, accounts receivable

Peter Kargard: music

Anna Kaufman: stenographer

Alfred Kaye: groceries, malted milk machine/lunch counter

Catherine Kehoe: switchboard operator

Jeff Kehoe: office boy

John Kehoe: sporting goods and hardware
Ralph Keller: office manager
Ed Kellner: butcher
Bob Kelly: delivery
Mark Kerski: office boy
Monica Kerski: lingerie, ladies ready-to-wear
Bob Kiefer: paint and wallpaper
Joe Kiefer: paint and wallpaper
Ed Kieff: men's furnishings
Joseph Kieff: domestics
Madeline Kieff: jewelry and silverware
Elizabeth Kiel: lunch counter
Jim Kiel: crockery
Esther King: secretary, office
George Kingston: watchman
Muriel Kirby: office
Dorothy Kitzinger: secretary, candy
June Klaver: drugs
Lucille Klaver: fabrics, notions, lingerie
Gary Klein: warehouse
Dawn Knutson: lunch counter
Dan Koehler: jewelry and silverware
Wilma Koehler: electrical and appliances
Marion Kohrt: stationery/cameras
Dorothy Kopetsky: jewelry, drugs
Joseph Kopetsky: domestics, linens, lingerie/pajamas, personnel
Verda Kopetsky: doughnut machine
Ceil Konyn: gift wrap
Clara Korinek: stenographer
Lydia (Podolski) Krajewski: office
Joseph Kramer: drugs
Eddie Krasnicky: paint and wallpaper
Edna Kraus: domestics
Gene Krause: office boy
Ray Kreziminski: furniture warehouse
Kenny Krouth: electrical and appliances

Ann Krozell: paint and wallpaper
Barbara Krueger: drugs
Erv Krukowski: floor coverings
Joan Krukowski: pharmacy, candy
James Kuehl: wholesale
Jean (Beyer) Kuehnau: handkerchiefs, scarves, gloves
Melvin Kuehnau: furniture
Adolph Kuhr: wholesale traffic manager
Loren Kuich: paint and wallpaper
Sophie Kuntz: switchboard operator
Carl Kussling: meats
Lois LaBombard: salesclerk
Marion LaFond: domestics
Gertrude LaFountain: domestics
Les LaFountain: floor coverings
Svea Lahoie: notions
Carl Landree: sporting goods, hardware, electrical and appliances
Mary Ann (Delfosse) Langell: groceries
A. J. Langer: furniture
Ethel Langer: grocery, gloves/scarves
Dorothy Langlois: shoes
Francis "Bucky" Langrill: pharmacy
Geneva LaPierre: salesclerk
Larry LaPierre: men's furnishings
Eleanor LaPlant: lunch counter
Agnes Larson: groceries
Anna Larson: draperies
Axel Larson: delivery
Dick Larson (father): delivery
Dick Larson (son): floor coverings
Ethel Larson: groceries
Ethel Larson: foundations, draperies
Florence "Flossie" Larson: kitchen supplies/housewares
Glen Larson: delivery
Ray Larson: delivery
Sonny Larson: maintenance
Jeannine Lascelle: cashier

Marlene Lascelle: credit
Chris Lauerman: office boy
Dorothy Lauerman: stationery/ cameras
Frank Lauerman Jr.: jewelry and silverware
Frank Lauerman III: music, hearing aids
Henry Lauerman Sr.: store president
Henry Lauerman Jr.: sporting goods and hardware
Jay (Frank IV) Lauerman: maintenance
Jim Lauerman: ladies' ready-to-wear
Joseph P. Lauerman: wholesale
Lynn Lauerman: stationery/cameras
Edward LaVoy: wholesale, piece goods
Kelly Law: electrical/appliances
Bob Laysell: electrical and appliances
Bruce Leannah: warehouse, cameras, stationery, toys, cards/gifts, school/ office supplies
Francis X. Leannah: cameras, stationery, toys, cards/gifts, school/ office supplies, crockery, religious items, gift wrap
Mike Leannah: music
Millie Leannah: stationery, toys
Patrick Leannah: floor coverings
Les LeBouton: cashier
Jess Legault: office manager, comptroller
Jeff Lehmann: music
Bertha Lemieux: jewelry and silverware
Wesley Lieburn: stock clerk
Adolph Limmert: floor coverings
P. J. Linden: shoes
Martha Lindlof: lunch counter, "doughnut lady"
Jake Lindsay: elevator operator
Joe Liska: sign painter
Lillian Lison: ladies' ready-to-wear
Charles Logan: shoes

Violet Loose: fabrics, notions
Mary (Dupuis) Losier: office
Tom Lund: paint and wallpaper
Selma Lupine: clerk
Agnes (Disch) Maas: infants' clothing
Julia Mack: cashier/green stamps
Anna Mae (Grenier) Madsen: ladies' ready-to-wear
Dan Madsen: electrical and appliances
Dorothy Madsen: domestics
Erma Madsen: gift wrap
Louis Magnuson: butcher
Luella Maske: salesclerk
Marge Mattson: religious items and gifts
Dutch Manderfield: furniture
Fran Marineau: toys
Luella Maske: salesclerk
Mary Mathy: stationery, crockery
Susan (Leannah) McAllister: cameras, stationery, gift wrap
Steve McBride: paint and wallpaper
Beatrice McCarthy: ladies' ready-to-wear
Flo McDermott: stationery, office/ school supplies
Mike McGowan: furntiture
Patrick McGowan: paints
Dick McKenney: electrical and appliance repair
Mae Mechalson: draperies
Barb Menard: cameras, cards
Woody Menard: toys warehouse
Arthur J. Menor: electrical and appliances
Isabel Menor: electrical and appliances
Margaret Menor: housewares
Marianne Menor: secretary
Karen Menza: religious items and gifts
Janet Merritt: stationery
Edward Meyers: crockery
Faye Meyers: children's clothing

Milt Meyers: furniture
Sidney Meyers: stock clerk
Ernie Miller: men's wear
Wayne Mills: notions, domestics, jewelry and silverware
Ann Modschiedler: lingerie
Martha Mogensen: domestics
Ida Morois: meats, wholesale
Linda Morois: lunch counter
May Mulholland: saleswoman
Jerry Murphy: ladies' hosiery and lingerie
Jim Murphy: warehouse, stationery, cameras, crockery
Joseph Murphy: linens, children's wear
Tom Myers: carpeting
Evelyn Nault: secretary
Doris Neargarth: advertising
Art Nelson: men's furnishings
Darlene Nelson: cameras, cards
Scott Nerat: floor coverings
Victor Neshek: hardware
Charles Neumeier: interior decorations/display
Patricia Newton: clerk
Leo Nice: paint and wallpaper
Janet Nicklaus: pharmacy
Mark Noel: paint and wallpaper
Ethel Nordin: secretary
Manette Nordin: switchboard operator
Stella Norton: clerk
Jerry Nowakowski: shoes
Mary Nowakowski: cashier, linens, shoes
Edith Nystrom: grocery
Margaret O'Connell: lingerie
Barbara Olsen: salesclerk
Beatrice Olsen: ladies' ready-to-wear
Virginia Olsen: domestics
Art Olson: hardware
Carl Olson: music
Monica Olson: music

Joe Osier: elevator operator
Leonard Ott: music
Martin Ourada: wholesale
Lloyd Paige: fire stoker
Judy Palladeau: ladies' ready-to-wear
Wilbert Panske: paint and wallpaper, warehouse
Norm Paque: butcher
Albert Parent: men's work clothing
Arthur Parent: men's furnishings
Dorothy Parent: notions, ladies handkerchiefs and gloves
Edith Parent: cashier
Edna Parent: doughnuts/malted milk machine
Laura Parent: jewelry and silverware
Dave Paris: floor coverings
Fred Paris: maintenance
Vi Parker: toys
Eleanor Parkinson: shoes
Mardee Parkinson: elevator operator
Edith Parthie: meat, groceries, cashier/green stamps
Lenore Parthie: salesclerk
Blanche Patterson: shoes, lunch counter
Bonnie Paulsen: hosiery/lingerie
Andrew Payant: men's alterations
Bud Payne: maintenance
Allan Pearson: salesclerk
Elizabeth Pearson: cashier
Tom Pender: carpeting, drapery
Helen Pepin: domestics
Edward Perso: linens
Billy Peters: shoes
Blackie Peters: delivery
C. L. "Louis" Peters: stationery, toys, office supplies, crockery, glassware, novelties, cameras, photographic equipment
Joy Peters: cashier

Nathalie (DeGaynor) Peters: hardware, electrical, cashier/green stamps

Howard Peterson: paint and wallpaper

Tom Peterson: paint and wallpaper

Barbara Pfaffl: drugs

Art Pfeiffer: wholesale (men's furnishings), retail (men's goods)

Frank Pfiester: wholesale, delivery

Leona Pfiester: infants' clothing, lingerie

Walter Pfiester: maintenance

Myron Phalen: salesclerk

Barb Pierce: secretary

Harold Pierce: children's clothing, lingerie, linens

Ray Pinkowski: domestics, candy, lunch counter, sewing machines, interior decorations/display, etc.

Alice Piontek: crockery cashier

Edith Place: stationery, office/school supplies

Helen Place: shoes

Leroy Pleshek: clerk

Marion Plouff: ladies' ready-to-wear

Thomas Plouff: ladies' ready-to-wear, millinery

Leo Podolski: paint and wallpaper

Steve Podolski: paint and wallpaper, warehouse

Janet Pogrant: secretary, jewelry and silverware

Helen Poquette: office

Lloyd Poquette: carpeting installation

Mavis Poquette: cashier

Sandy Poquette: electrical and appliances

Bill Porter: warehouse receiving clerk

Ann Powers: salesclerk

Bina Powers: groceries/cookies

Al Pristelski: children's clothing, lingerie

Byron Raab: paint and wallpaper

Millie "Babe" (Pelner) Raboin: drapery maker/upholstery, office

Josephine Racine: salesclerk

Helen Rademacher: ladies' ready-to-wear

Wally Rademacher: floor coverings

William Rader: maintenance

Bill Ramsay: accounts payable

Viola Ramsay: switchboard operator

Evelyn Raygo: lunch counter

Herb Raygo: furniture

Ken Raygo: drapery installer

Theresa Raymaker: salesclerk

Jeff Reiswitz: printing

Dave Remmington: furniture, floor coverings

Janet (Jensen) Remmington: housewares, elevator operator, gift wrap, toys

Rick Remmington: maintenance

Lorraine Renton: gloves/neckwear, candy, infants' clothing, draperies (buyer), lingerie, gift wrap

Clarence Retlick: stock clerk

George Retlick: furniture repair, warehouse

Margaret Retlick: gift wrap

Sam Reynoldson: paint and wallpaper

Ember Rickaby: lunch counter

Orphan Riley: salesclerk

Roland Rittich: music

Shirley Roberts: office

Doris Roeder: maintenance

Helen Roehl: stationery/cameras

Edna Rogge: stenographer, office credit manager

Pat Rondeau: office/school supplies

George Roosen: butcher

Dan Ross: hardware

Rose Ruby: domestics

Jackie Rudolph: children's clothing

Kim Rudolph: furniture, warehouse

Violet Runke: office
Ellen Rynish-Olsen: stationery, office/ school supplies
Lila Sadowski: candy
Rita Sadowski: linens, lunch counter
Don St. Cyr: credit office
Geri St. Dennis: secretary, furniture
Harold St. Dennis: carpeting, furniture
Joe St. Thomas: groceries
Inez Samuelson: seamstress, upholstery/draperies
Tim Saxton: maintenance
Adrienne Schacht: fabrics, notions
George Schacht: men's overalls and gloves
Rueben Schacht: women's shoes, luggage
Christian Scheldt: salesclerk
Joanne Schiller: drugs
Mildred Schimke: salesclerk
James J. Schleihs: tobacco counter
Mathilda "Tillie" Schmidt: ladies' ready-to-wear
Dick Schneider: shipping clerk
Dorothy Schneider: lingerie
Wilbur Schomaker: Santa Claus
Claudia Schramm: salesclerk
Evelyn Schreiner: salesclerk
Charlotte Schroeder: lunch counter
Myrtle Schroeder: foundations
Dorothy Schuchart: salesclerk
Marion Schuchart: secretary
Emmie Schussler: cameras, cards
Arlene Schultz: office
Betty Schultz: stationery
Elizabeth Scott: salesclerk
Fae Seefeldt: furniture, drapery maker
Doris Seibt: lunch counter
George Seymour: paint and wallpaper
Charlotte Shake: ready-to-wear
Curt Shaver: office boy

Jen Shaver: crockery
Helen Shefky: office, charge sales
Bonita Shehow: hosiery
Connie Shepro: housewares
Irvin Shepro: sporting goods and hardware
Ervin Sigloff: shoes
Donna Sindler: lingerie
Rueben Singer: butcher
Betty Sladek: payroll
Eleanor Sladky: office
Cindy Smith: electrical and appliances
Bea Snyder: ladies' ready-to-wear
Dick Soderberg: electrical and appliances
Signa Soderberg: housewares
Ted Soderberg: electrical and appliances
Marjorie Sorenson: crockery
Tillie Sotka: paint and wallpaper
Felix Stang: delivery
Imelda Stang: ladies' ready-to-wear, millinery
John Stanish: hardware
Norma Stauber: jewelry and silverware, furniture
Al Steffen: music, sewing machines
Marge Stephenson: ladies' ready-to-wear
Mathilda Stromer: groceries/cash and carry
Charlotte Strutz: domestics
Dennis Sulk: delivery
Diane (Eland) Sulk: lunch counter
Lenroy Sulk: maintenance
Sonny Sulk: wholesale
Betty (Klaver) Sundstrom: children's clothing, linens
Nat Swain: electrical and appliances
Clifford Swanson: butcher
Carla Tanguay: lunch counter, candy
Elsie Tansey: domestics

Eleanor Tebo: groceries, telephone orders

Mark Techmeier: music

Louie Tharp: lunch counter

Vic Thedick: security

Cindy Theis: stationery, office/school supplies

Florence Theis: paint and wallpaper

Larry Thomson: furniture, electrical and appliances, warehouse

Ella Thoreson: stenographer

Marie Thull: secretary

Vi Thull: religious items and gifts

Bob Thyberg: jewelry, credit

Burl "Pato" Thyne: maintenance

Pete Thyne: printing

Les Topel: printing

Ellen Topel: office

Darlene Trautner: jewelry, shoes

Dean Tremblay: maintenance

Sue Tremblay: electrical and appliances

Lucille Trottier: lingerie

Laverne Tupper: groceries, housewares

Sue Uecke: advertising

Jack Valictka: butcher

Patricia Vandenbranden: sales

Jim Van Hemelryk: delivery

Jean Vedra: music

Henry Vennix: lamps, furniture/draperies

John Victor: shoes and luggage

Mary Victor: groceries

Millie Vieth: paint and wallpaper

Emil Voscamp: men's furnishings, suits and coats

James Wachal: stock

Claire Wagner: shoes

George Wagner, Jr.: crockery

Gerald Walk: stock clerk

Nathalie Walk: billing

Sandy Walker: paint and wallpaper

Clarence Watkins: sewing machines, "Singer dept."

Gus Waugus: elevator operator, maintenance

Pat (Cisco) Waugus: stenographer

Don Wauters: floor coverings

Duane Wauters: floor coverings

Bernadette Weber: bookkeeper, payroll

Curt Weber: sporting goods and hardware

Gert Weber: office

Maude Weigert: cashier, ladies' ready-to-wear

Helen Weiler: clerk

Patricia Weir: clerk

Frank Wells: furniture

Vern Wenzel: music/antenna installation

Betty Wertepny: paint and wallpaper

Juanita White: salesclerk

Walter White: music, warehouse for children's clothing, lingerie

Carl Widen: shoes

James Widen: salesclerk

Lawrence Williams: upholstery

Austin M. Wilson: jewelry, art goods, fancy work (knitting and embroidery)

Jack Wilson: ladies' ready-to-wear

George Winnekins: men's furnishings

Kay Wolverton: drugs

Clara Woods: hosiery

Lucille Woods: hosiery

Janet Wozniak: office

Mary Wright: draperies, foundations, hosiery

Roger Wuhrman: paint and wallpaper

Tim Wuhrman: furniture

Earl Younk: butcher

Kay Yunke: drugs

Carol Zebrasky: fabrics, notions

Last Word

WALTER DEVOE started working at Lauerman Brothers Department Store in 1911. More than sixty years later, he gave a small speech at his retirement party. In the midst of that speech he uttered the following words: "I love every brick in the building."

Walter DeVoe doesn't stand alone in his feelings for Lauermans.

And there are a great number of bricks in that building.

Index